THE MANUAL OF

TANK
BUSTERS

THE MANUAL OF
TANK BUSTERS

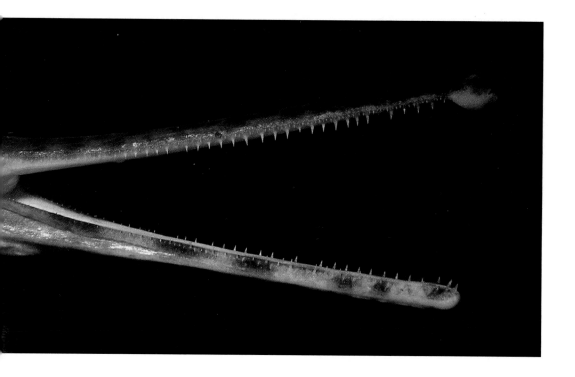

GINA SANDFORD
RICHARD CROW

a Salamander book

Published by Salamander Books Limited
LONDON • NEW YORK

A SALAMANDER BOOK

ISBN 0 86101 473 1

Distributed in the UK by
Hodder and Stoughton Services,
P.O. Box 6, Mill Road, Dunton Green,
Sevenoaks, Kent TN13 2XX.

CREDITS

Created by Ideas into Print
Designed by Jill Coote
Colour reproductions: Magnum Graphics Ltd.
Typeset by SX Composing Ltd.
Printed in Singapore

THE AUTHORS

Gina Sandford's interest in fishes began with a
goldfish and developed to include sticklebacks,
young perch, pike and, eventually, tropical fish.
She has kept and bred many species, but has a
particular love for catfishes and the osteoglossids.
She has written for magazines and journals, and
travels widely, giving audio-visual presentations
and lectures. She is Secretary and Editor for the
Catfish Association of Great Britain.

Richard Crow, who has written the cichlid
section, started keeping tropical fish in 1971. After
creating a purpose-built fish house, home at one
point to over 3,000 young cichlids, he bred many
cichlid species, including over 27 species of
Cichlasoma. He has written countless articles for
magazines and associations and was Editor of the
British Cichlid Association in 1985-1988.

Consultants: Dr. Keith Banister, Heiko Bleher.

Half-title page: A young specimen of Hemisorubim
platyrhynchus, *destined to reach 35.5cm(14in).*
Title page: The distinctive snout of the longnose gar,
Lepisosteus osseus, *bristling with tiny teeth.*
This page: The pacu, Piaractus brachypomum,
lives on fruit and seeds in its native South America.

CONTENTS

PRACTICAL MATTERS

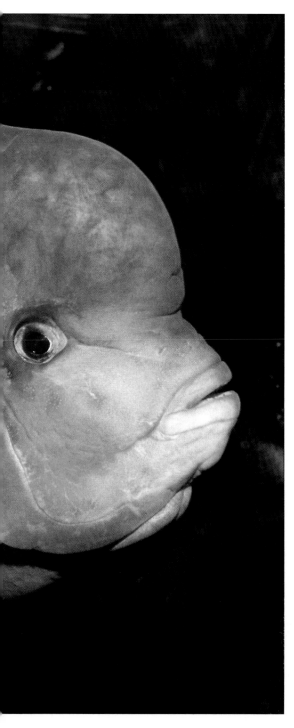

It is always difficult to know where to start when planning a new aquarium. The temptation is to buy a fish first and then consider the problems of housing it. Misjudging the long-term implications is easy, especially if the specimen you have chosen is a juvenile. After all, it shouldn't grow that fast – you hope!

Like any other animal, large fishes need adequate accommodation, regular feeding, clean conditions and appropriate exercise. In fact, you should always give as much consideration to owning a fish as you would to owning a dog or a horse.

Having decided on a fish that interests you, the first task is to determine the minimum tank size it will need. Next, investigate the ideal filtration system to maintain the required water conditions. A filter system can never be too large for the aquarium; however big the tank, it is nowhere near the size of the lake or river in which the fish lives in the wild. Lighting and heating options and the feeding strategies of the fish are the next priorities. When you have established these, you can consider where to site the tank. The choice of external tank decor is entirely up to you, but inside the aquarium you must consider the fish's requirements as well as your own personal taste. The early chapters of this book will help you resolve all these questions, but only when the tank is set up and has been running for at least a month should you consider buying the fish.

One thing is certain; at some stage in your fishkeeping career, you will encounter problems. To help you, a brief description of some of the more common fish ailments and their treatment is given in the chapter on basic health care. Remember, there are no easy routes to successful fishkeeping. In your journey of discovery, patience and experience will play a major role; this opening section is simply to start you off in the right direction.

Left: *A fine* Cichlasoma synspilum, *one of the most colourful and popular of the large cichlids available to the fishkeeping hobby.*

SETTING UP THE AQUARIUM

When installing any aquarium, whatever its size, there are a number of important points to consider. Many of these revolve around the tank itself – what size to choose or construct, how to support it, where to position it in the room (both in terms of its relation to ambient light and access to electrical points, etc.), and what heating, lighting and filtration systems to install. All of these factors inevitably reflect the most important decision of all – what fish do you wish to keep? In this opening section, we review the practicalities of setting up an aquarium suitable for the larger fish featured in the book.

Choosing an aquarium

When you opt for a certain size of aquarium, bear in mind how big your fish are likely to grow, and if you are buying subadult or mature fish, use a large aquarium from the outset. Many large fish have very fast growth rates, particularly in the first year, and it is better both for the juvenile fish and for yourself if your fish do not have to be moved too frequently as they outgrow a series of smaller tanks. Also bear in mind that the width of the aquarium – the distance from the front to the rear glass – should be sufficient to allow the fully grown fish to turn easily.

The choice of aquariums is wide, from all-glass models – some with bowed front glass – to those constructed with an acrylic material that allows welded seams and tanks of infinite length and depth. The choice is up to you. Invariably, the best choice is an all-glass tank, as this will prove both the cheapest and easiest option. The minimum tank size for keeping large mature fish is 2m(79in) long by 75cm(30in) wide and 75cm deep. You can ask your dealer to arrange for this to be made and he should be willing to deliver it for you. (Tanks over 2.5m/8.2ft long usually have to be constructed in situ.) Ensure that new glass of sufficient thickness is used in its construction, at least 12mm(0.5in) thick for a

Below: *This attractive large aquarium literally provides a 'window' into the underwater world. The life-support systems are located underneath.*

2m tank that is 75cm deep, and 18mm(0.7in) thick if it is 1m(39in) deep. Sometimes, cheaper tanks are offered for sale that have been made from secondhand glass, perhaps having seen long service as shop windows. These are often of inferior quality. The stresses set up by the effects of heat and cold on the glass could have weakened it to the point that it may fracture under pressure in a full aquarium.

Assembling your own aquarium
It is best to construct large aquariums in situ, otherwise they can be difficult to lift and manipulate into position. Indeed, it may be impossible to get an assembled tank through the door, and while it has been known for aquarists to remove window frames in order to pass a tank through, this is not an idea to be recommended!

If you are assembling an all-glass tank yourself, it is best to leave the cutting of the

***Above:** Well-designed and suitably located tanks can make excellent* *room features. Note the sturdy brickwork that supports the tank.*

individual sheets to a professional glazier. With a bit of practice, it is fairly easy to cut glass up to 6mm(0.24in) thick; 12mm thick glass is altogether a different matter. Let the glazier know the exact sizes of the glass panels you require for your aquarium, and be sure to ask for ground edges for safety. Should any mistakes occur in the cutting of the glass, make sure they are not of your making; let the glazier absorb the cost of the error. Glass, particularly in the thicknesses required here, is very expensive.

Before ordering the glass panels, bear in mind the overall design of the aquarium and associated systems. For example, if you envisage incorporating an overflow system to supply an undertank gravity-fed rapid sand filter, you will need a suitable hole in one of the side walls of the aquarium. If this is required, again use the services of a professional glazier; suitable drills are exceedingly expensive, and one small mistake could be very costly.

Once the panes are cut, assembling an all-glass aquarium is fairly straightforward, using silicone rubber sealant to join the panes of glass together and create a watertight seal. The main problem, however, is the sheer scale of the tank. For the heavy lifting work you will need the assistance of two strong people; handling large sheets of glass is difficult and holding them in position while the silicone sealant sets can be fraught with danger.

Always take suitable safety measures and maintain them during the construction of a large tank. Make sure that children and pets are well out of the way, for example, and use the correct posture when lifting heavy materials; glass is heavy, and needs to be treated with respect. Bear in mind that a bare tank of 2mx75x75cm(79x30x30in) constructed from 12mm(0.5in) thick glass will weigh about 176kg(388lb). (When water and decoration is added, such a set up will weigh more than 1,250kg/2,750lb.) Ensure that the room is well ventilated when you use the silicone sealant. This gives off heavy soporific fumes during curing and can be particularly potent when you lean over the aquarium to apply the inside seals.

Large glass aquariums need to have sufficient strengtheners running along the length and at regular intervals across the width at the top to counteract the bowing effect of the water pressure at the centre of the tank. Arrange these stiffeners and braces so that they do not impede access to the tank, as this will cause problems when you introduce large rocks or wood, as well as proving a barrier should you have to move large fish.

Before decorating the tank, fill it with water to check for any leaks. This is just as important with ready-made tanks as it is with homemade versions – while the manufacturer may have checked the tank before selling it to you, the seal may have been fractured in transit. It is far easier to remove clean water and dry the tank out before resealing than to remove tank decoration and gravel as well.

Constructing a large aquarium (2m×75cm×75cm/79×30×30in)

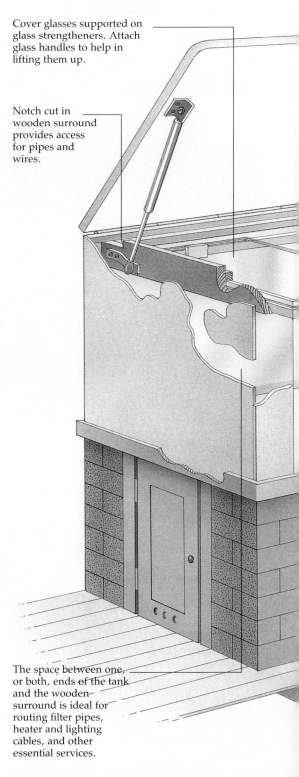

Cover glasses supported on glass strengtheners. Attach glass handles to help in lifting them up.

Notch cut in wooden surround provides access for pipes and wires.

The space between one, or both, ends of the tank and the wooden surround is ideal for routing filter pipes, heater and lighting cables, and other essential services.

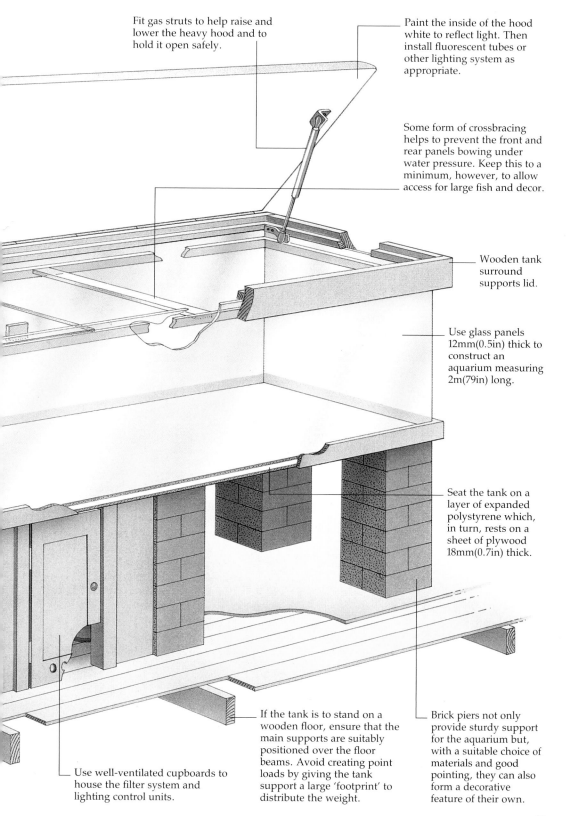

Fit gas struts to help raise and lower the heavy hood and to hold it open safely.

Paint the inside of the hood white to reflect light. Then install fluorescent tubes or other lighting system as appropriate.

Some form of crossbracing helps to prevent the front and rear panels bowing under water pressure. Keep this to a minimum, however, to allow access for large fish and decor.

Wooden tank surround supports lid.

Use glass panels 12mm(0.5in) thick to construct an aquarium measuring 2m(79in) long.

Seat the tank on a layer of expanded polystyrene which, in turn, rests on a sheet of plywood 18mm(0.7in) thick.

Use well-ventilated cupboards to house the filter system and lighting control units.

If the tank is to stand on a wooden floor, ensure that the main supports are suitably positioned over the floor beams. Avoid creating point loads by giving the tank support a large 'footprint' to distribute the weight.

Brick piers not only provide sturdy support for the aquarium but, with a suitable choice of materials and good pointing, they can also form a decorative feature of their own.

Using acrylic instead of glass

An alternative to glass is a transparent acrylic material, which has the advantage of being light, strong and can be welded to give a seamless finish to the aquarium. Its main disadvantage is that it scratches more readily than glass, so always take extra care when removing algae to ensure that no particles of sand or gravel are trapped between the cleaner and the acrylic surface. Its greatest advantage is that it can be used as a curved viewing panel to a large concrete vat of the type used by large public aquariums. Here, it can be drilled, seated on a rubberized sealing layer and bolted into place on the inside of the tank. When the tank is filled, the water pressure then completes the seal. This technique is extremely useful if you are constructing a concrete pond for your fish in the conservatory, as it allows a viewing panel in the side of a raised pond.

Cover glasses

Order the cover glasses at the same time as the tank, and ensure that they are substantial enough to avoid being damaged by jumping fish. Use silicone sealant to attach marbles or smaller pieces of glass to the cover glasses at the front and back to act as handles so that you can lift them out and clean them easily.

Three or even four cover glasses are ideal. Having several cover glasses gives you the opportunity to work on one section of the aquarium at a time – when carrying out regular maintenance, for example – while maintaining a cover on the remainder of the aquarium to prevent any nervous fishes from jumping out. In this connection, introducing floating plants such as water lettuce (*Pistia stratiotes*) appears to prevent fishes leaping out. It seems that the plants give the fish a clear indication of where the water surface is and, when frightened, they tend to retire beneath a clump of plants rather than leap from the water.

Clean the cover glasses regularly to prevent a build-up of algae and salts that could cut down light reaching the plants. Cover glasses can be dispensed with altogether if the fish can be held in check, although then there may be problems with the rapid evaporation of water.

Tank stands

If you are building a tank in situ, it is vital to consider the siting and construction of the stand before starting on the aquarium. Although traditional metal stands are available from your dealer, they are often not strong enough to support larger aquariums. Indeed, the size you require will probably not be a stock item and you will need to order a specially constructed stand at the same time as you order the aquarium.

However, there are many alternatives open to you. Decorative brick piers are an ideal way of supporting an aquarium, and you can incorporate cupboards for power filters or filtration tanks, time switches and lighting control gear, etc., between them. The doors sold for kitchen units are ideal for filling the gaps between piers, and are available in a wide variety of finishes to match your room decor. Always ensure that there is a good flow of air into the cupboards to avoid the build-up of condensation if they enclose a biological filter system.

Before placing the tank on the piers, place a sheet of marine plywood or similar material, at least 18mm(0.7in) thick and the same size as the base of the aquarium, across the piers. Lay a thick sheet of expanded polystyrene between the tank and the wood to absorb any small imperfections or undulations in the surface of the wood. Even a small unevenness can cause the base of an aquarium to split when the full pressure of water is applied to it.

You can also use wood to construct the stand, but remember that timber is prone to rotting, especially if subjected to the humidity created by an open trickle filter system. And be careful about using wood preservatives; the chemicals used in some preservatives are highly toxic and could be detrimental to your fish. The best strategy is to seal the wood with a clear varnish and allow this to dry completely before installing the aquarium and filtration system. You can also use wood cladding around the sides of the aquarium to improve its appearance as a piece of furniture.

Wherever you decide to put your aquarium, always check that the floor is capable of taking the weight. This is especially important in rooms with timber floors. The total loading should be evenly spread *across* the floor beams (these run at 90° to the floorboards). If this is not possible then ensure that the load bearing points are directly above the floor beams and not on the thinner floorboards. Always try to spread the load of the aquarium over the greatest number of supports, avoiding excessive loads at any specific point.

In choosing your ideal location from a structural point of view also try to site the aquarium where the fish are not going to be disturbed or frightened by any sudden movements caused by children, pets or deranged friends and neighbours.

Aquarium hoods

If your aquarium is destined to have a hood then it will need to be constructed of timber to match the cladding of the tank or the doors used in the stand, or of metal. Make sure there is sufficient clearance between the hood and the cover glasses to enable it to house the fluorescent tubes (see the section on lighting). The interior surface of

Below: Blending a large aquarium with the room decor not only creates a pleasing effect but also disguises the high-tech support system required.

the hood should reflect light back into the aquarium. This can be achieved by lining it with aluminium foil (carefully stuck to the wood), painting it white or making it out of white-faced boards.

Because of the sheer size of a large aquarium, the hood will be heavy and cumbersome to move. One option is to hinge the hood to the aquarium cabinet and devise a method of propping it open safely so that one person can carry out any routine work needed on the tank. Where the hood is a one-piece removable structure, you may need assistance to remove it when servicing the tank and, in times of emergencies, this help may not be available. Separate hoods in sections may well prove the answer. Another alternative is to dispense with the hood altogether, using suspended metal halide, mercury vapour or similar lamps to illuminate the aquarium. This is an option discussed in the lighting section.

Indoor pools

If you have a fish house or a conservatory, the answer to keeping large fishes could be an indoor pool. The easiest type to construct is a raised pond, using breeze blocks or concrete blocks, rendered with cement and

treated with a sealant to prevent lime leaching into the water – exactly the way you would construct a garden pond. Alternatively, line the block shell with a butyl rubber pond liner. Incorporate shallow areas and ledges so that you can grow tropical water plants in conditions similar to their native environment. These shallow areas may also provide spawning grounds for the fishes. Incorporate a suitable filtration system beside the pool, either in a cupboard or as an open feature with plants growing in the top. Face the exterior of the pool with brick, wood or stone to create a decorative and functional finish. It is quite easy to provide planting areas in the surrounding wall to display terrestrial plants and flowers.

Heating the aquarium or pool
It is always difficult to decide on the exact heating requirements for an aquarium, mainly because there are so many external factors to take into account. Is the room heated, for example? Does this heating go off at night? In an unheated outhouse, what are the minimum night temperatures likely to be? The recommendations given here are simply a guide. The only way of ensuring that the correct temperature requirements are being met is to run the tank and monitor it for several weeks. For large tanks in a normal room environment, the average heating requirements will be about 1 watt per litre(4.5 watts per gallon). This figure can double for a pond or a tank in an unheated conservatory or one with an uncovered top.

Modern heaters and thermostats are very reliable. The choice between combined heater/thermostats or separate units is up to the individual (and a question of availability in some countries). Heater/thermostats have the advantage of being easier to install, just requiring connection to the power supply. (Even here, though, be sure to distinguish between completely submersible and semi-submersible models.) It makes good sense to use two, or even three heater/thermostats of lower wattage than a single unit of the required wattage, and to set the thermostats at slightly different temperatures. This ensures that should one stick on, i.e. continue to heat up past the set

temperature, the others will cut out. A single heater of lower wattage than required will be unable to raise the water temperature to such a degree that the fish will suffer. On the other hand, should one heater fail to come on, the remaining ones will ensure that the temperature does not fall to a dangerous level. However, both increases and decreases in temperature in large volumes of water are much slower than in smaller aquariums. When using more than one heating unit, place them at either ends of the aquarium to give an even spread of heat, although the flow from the filtration system should spread the warmed water throughout the aquarium.

Large fishes are notorious for their ability to break heaters and thermostats, either by flicking them against the sides of the aquarium with their body movements or by picking them up in their mouths and dashing them against rocks as they strive to redecorate the aquarium in a style more pleasing to themselves! One way of avoiding this is to section off the rear corners of the aquarium with pieces of glass and place the heaters and filtration pipes behind these panels. Leave a gap at the top and bottom to allow free circulation of water over the heater elements. Alternatively, if you have opted for a separate biological filter system, you can incorporate the heating elements in the filter tank. This serves two purposes: it prevents fishes from breaking the heaters and also removes the need for unsightly wires in the main aquarium. Using this arrangement, the water is filtered, aerated and heated in the filtration system and then pumped into the aquarium. If this is an impractical solution, wrap the heater loosely in plastic mesh to prevent inquisitive or boisterous fish from damaging either themselves or the heaters.

For indoor pools, consider using metal pond heaters. You may encounter problems with catfishes, for example, that persist in lying close to the heater, thus sustaining burns on their flanks, something they are prone to do with glass heaters in the aquarium. To overcome this, use the piece of expanded polystyrene supplied with the heater to enable it to float freely in the pool. A little unsightly, perhaps, but nonetheless an effective solution.

Above: A pool of 4,100 litres(900 gallons) in a conservatory. A foam pond filter and the warmth of summer provide ideal conditions for keeping a wide range of large fish species.

Left: In this aquarium lighting system note that the electrical connections are located safely on the other side of the white baffle, the endcaps are waterproof and the tubes covered with a protective mesh in case of breakage.

Lighting the aquarium or pool

The amount of lighting required for the aquarium will depend on the effect you wish to create. The deeper the aquarium, the more intense lighting you will need to penetrate to the substrate. This high degree of lighting will only be required if you are intending to grow plants in the substrate.

The most popular way of lighting the aquarium is with fluorescent tubes. On a 2mx75cmx75cm(79inx30inx30in) aquarium, use at least four 80w tubes in a combination of various colours, including a balanced daylight tube and a 'pink' plant growth-enhancing tube among them. If your aquarium has a hood then install these tubes in the normal way, holding them in place with clips and using waterproof end caps. It is best to accommodate all the control units outside the hood. This not only cuts down the build-up of heat in the limited space between the cover glasses and the hood, but also avoids running electrical control gear in a damp environment. If you have to accommodate the starter units within the hood, ensure that there is sufficient air flow through the hood to disperse the heat.

Ideally, control the start up and close down sequence of the lights with time switches so that they come on and go off in stages, say one tube every 20 minutes, giving the highest light intensity over the greater part of the day. If you are trying to imitate the tropical day, time the lighting to be on for 12 hours and off for 12 hours.

As fluorescent tubes run relatively cool, there is no scorching of the leaves of floating plants. And with four tubes over

the aquarium it should be possible to grow plants such as Java fern (*Microsorium pteropus*) attached to the wood or rocks. However, if you aspire to nurturing specimen Amazon sword plants (*Echinodorus* sp.) in the substrate then you will need a more intense lighting system to penetrate a water depth of 75cm(30in). In this case, you will need to consider using spot lights or the more powerful mercury vapour or metal halide lamps that are available under a variety of trade names.

Spot lights may be wall mounted or suspended over the aquarium so that they are about 30cm(12in) above the water surface. They are ideal for accentuating features within the aquarium, such as a specimen plant or decorative piece of wood. The spread of light from spots is limited, so the addition of fluorescent tubes at the front and rear of the tank will give a more even spread of illumination. (Be very careful about using tungsten spotlamps too near the water surface. It is a question of achieving a compromise between siting them close enough to provide useful lighting effects and positioning them safely out of the 'splash zone'. At any rate, consider using cover glasses if you are in any doubt about the safety of your lighting

Above: *Use spotlights to create bright areas in the foreground of the tank* *(left). In the right-hand tank, plants thrive under similar suspended lights.*

system.) Mercury vapour and metal halide lamps are excellent sources of light, but they produce too much heat for them to be confined within an aquarium hood. The best way of using these lamps is to suspend them above the aquarium so that they are about 50cm(20in) above the water surface. Any lower and they will heat the surface layers of the water to the detriment of the fish. Where they throw pools of dappled light on the aquarium floor, the plants grow exceedingly well, and the darker regions provide the opportunity for seclusion that many fishes need in order to feel at ease in the aquarium. Again, infill lighting can be provided with fluorescent tubes. Use cover glasses on such an aquarium if you wish, but be sure to keep them free of algae, which grow very quickly in the bright, humid conditions.

Always ensure that these high-intensity lights cannot be viewed directly, and that they are adequately screened to prevent damage to your sight. This problem is not apparent to the fish, as the water effectively diffuses the sharpness of light they produce. These lamps are excellent over open pools and aquariums where plants develop emerse leaves and may eventually flower. Again, because of their high running temperatures, place them at least 50cm(20in) above the water surface; even at this height, the leaves of emerse and floating plants may be scorched.

Tying up loose ends

Once you have installed all the systems in your aquarium or pool, make sure that all the wiring and pipework is tidy. There is nothing more aggravating than trying to service a power filter and finding that all the wiring to the lighting system is tangled around the pipework to the filter. Not only is this annoying, but it can also be dangerous. To this end, cut all flexible hoses on filtration systems to suitable lengths and shorten excessively long wiring.

As far as electrical connections are concerned, there are a variety of control boxes available that enable you to connect the separate power leads to the lights, heaters and filters into a central box, which has a single cable to the mains supply. Should one of these boxes not meet your needs, ask a qualified electrician to design a unit to suit your specific requirements. Do not attempt to connect up any electrical equipment to an aquarium or pool if you feel unsure about the proper methods involved: water and electricity make a dangerous combination.

Choosing your fish

Once you have your aquarium system up and running, it is time to consider what fishes you would like to keep. The choice of potentially large fishes is vast. This book covers only the more commonly available species, but the basic rules apply to all fish. Reading through fishkeeping publications, you may come across a species that appeals to you but, at that particular time, it may not be readily available or so new to the trade and thus expensive that you think twice before taking the plunge. In any event, do as much background research as possible on any new species before you buy it, and to ensure that the aquarium filtration systems are properly installed and matured before you take delivery.

Perhaps you wish to keep a single specimen destined to become a household pet, complete with a name and pride of place as the centre of attraction. Or you may

Below: A stately oscar (Astronotus ocellatus) at home in a spacious aquarium. This cichlid from South America can become a personal 'pet'.

prefer to keep several fishes, such as the free-swimming tinfoil barb (*Barbus schwanenfeldi*) combined with more sedentary catfishes, or to foster a community of cichlids that will breed.

Once you have decided on the type of fish you wish to keep, you will need to choose between buying an adult specimen or a juvenile. Experience shows that juveniles are much easier to acclimatize to aquarium conditions than adults. There is also the added advantage that smaller specimens are cheaper to buy.

Buying and introducing your fish

When you buy your fish, do not be afraid to ask to see it feeding. Check what the shop owner is feeding it and make sure that you do the same, at least to start with. Look for signs of damage in transit – split fins are the most common. If the fish has been kept in good conditions, it will be alert, with good colour on the body and any split fins will be showing signs of healing.

Below: A fine giraffe catfish (Auchenoglanis occidentalis) *sifting the tank substrate for food. Youngsters are ideal to mix with midwater fish.*

If the dealer's conditions leave something to be desired, secondary fungal or bacterial infections may have set in. Unless you are an experienced aquarist, avoid buying any fish that show signs of disease or behave in an unusual manner, such as nervous twitching, sudden dashes around the aquarium, laying motionless on their side or breathing rapidly.

The usual method of transporting fish is in clear plastic bags. Depending on the distance to be travelled and the fish involved, the dealer may fill the bag with oxygen rather than air to sustain the fish during the journey. When you get home, float the bag in the aquarium to allow the water in the bag to reach the temperature of your tank water. Before releasing the fish, mix some of the aquarium water with that in the bag to accustom the fish to the new water. This process can take several hours if your water is very different from that of your supplier. If necessary, place the fish in a bucket with the water from the bag and some of the tank water and continue to trickle in the tank water slowly through a piece of airline. If the fish shows no sign of distress, place it in the aquarium.

Above: *This predatory tiger shovelnose catfish* (Pseudoplatystoma fasciatum) *can reach a length of 1.5m(5ft) and needs plenty of space.*

Below: *The same species as a youngster. Buying juveniles is the best approach, but it is vital to know the final size they will attain.*

It is best to transport large specimens, or those with sharp fin spines of scutes, in a bucket or in a large plastic bag within a polystyrene box. Transported in this way, with a larger volume of water, the temperature loss is usually only one or two degrees. As with small specimens, add tank water slowly to acclimatize the fish.

When introduced into the aquarium, most fish will either hide or sit on the bottom for a while before venturing out into their new surroundings. At this time, keep the lighting low and avoid any rapid movements near the tank. Allow the fish time to settle in; patience is the key. Sooner or later you will see it swimming around the aquarium or moving about from one sheltered spot to another. This process may take 30 minutes or several hours. Once the fish shows at least some activity, try a little food and then leave well alone.

If you intend to keep a community of large fish then it is best to buy them all at the same time as young specimens and grow them from the start in the large aquarium. Young fishes have not had the experience of setting up territories in the wild and defending them; in the aquarium, they become accustomed to each other as they set up their own territories for the first time. Provided that you do nothing foolish to change these territorial boundaries, such as moving a piece of wood, rock or a plant, they will live in harmony.

Sometimes, it is necessary to introduce a new fish into an established aquarium. If the resident fish are particularly territorial, the only relatively safe method is to break the above rule and deliberately rearrange the tank decoration so that all existing territorial boundaries are removed, then introduce the new fish. This ensures that they all start out on the same footing and have to establish new territories. Without making these changes, any new fish would be encroaching on another fish's previously established territory.

If you intend to keep only one or two specimen fish, house the youngsters initially in aquariums that are approximately 1mx50x50cm(39x20x20in). These tanks should be permanent installations with fully mature filtration systems, aged water and complete with plants. There are several reasons for this.

First, such a tank allows the new fish to be kept in quarantine. Should there be any disease problems or parasites, it is relatively easy to catch the fish and treat it elsewhere or treat it in situ, the relatively low volume of water requiring less medication than in the final show aquarium. The plants in the aquarium provide some seclusion and give the fish a sense of security lacking in a conventional bare quarantine tank. This reduces stress, often displayed by frightened fish as sudden violent dashes around the aquarium and rapid breathing.

Secondly, in a separate tank it is easier to check that the fish is feeding properly. It can be very difficult to persuade wild-caught and adult fishes to accept a new diet. Feeding patterns are not as well established in young fish, however, and thus it is easier to tempt a new acquisition with a variety of foods, at least some of which the fish will accept. Once the fish is feeding, half the battle is won. As it begins to grow and gain weight then you can begin to offer variations in diet. It is usual for juveniles to remain in their initial aquarium for six months and then be moved, while still at an easily manageable size, to their final tank.

Mature specimens, on the other hand, will need to be housed in the large aquarium from the start, and often will only accept a diet close to what they would find in the wild. This may need to include live fish in the first instance. If your conscience permits, offer live foods until the fish has accepted confinement in captivity and is putting on weight. Once settled, you can offer it more convenient alternatives, but be prepared for it to take some considerable time, maybe even months, before it will fully accept prepared foods.

The upheaval of moving house

Nowadays, moving house is a relatively common occurrence. This task is daunting enough, but combine it with moving livestock – especially fishes – and the thought is enough to make anyone stay where they are. Even a small community tank can become a major problem when most of the water has to be taken as well.

Moving large fishes needs careful planning. You must consider not only the move itself, but also what method you will use to catch and transport the fish – bags, boxes, buckets, or a water tank big enough to hold the fish – as well as adequate containers to take as much water as is practicable. Clearly, you also need to arrange for a vehicle big enough to carry all these items. If possible, arrange for access to the new premises a couple of days before the move so you can begin to transport extra water, rocks, woods, etc., in advance. Above all, allow plenty of time – moving always takes twice as long as you think.

When using nets to catch fish, ensure that they are made from a fine material that will not snag on fin spines and cause damage. For catching large fishes, consider using a net made from a linen pillowcase. This not only proves effective for moving spiny catfishes without fear of them damaging themselves, but is also equally useful for catching other species. The main key to its success is the size – the best dimensions being about 50cm(20in) long with an opening 30cm(12in) wide by 25cm(10in) high. To use such a net, lower the water level in the aquarium and remove any wood or rocks that the fish may damage themselves on should they take fright. Thoroughly soak the net in the water and hold it against the bottom of the aquarium while gently coaxing bottom-dwelling fish into it with your free hand. For midwater fish, adopt a similar method but hold the net higher in the water. Above all, do not bring the net up underneath a surface-dwelling fish; it causes them to panic and leap from the water. The length of the net allows you to close the top with your free hand as you remove it from the aquarium and thus prevent fish from jumping out. It is possible to catch fishes up to 30-40cm(12-16in) long using this method.

Above: *Transporting*   *The injured dorsal fin on*
fish can cause damage   *this catfish is vulnerable*
and subsequent infection.   *to fungi and bacteria.*

The one disadvantage of this net is its ability to hold water. Linen retains the water quite easily and it is often necessary to wait several minutes for some of it to drain away before trying to lift the net and fish from the aquarium, otherwise you tend to get rather wet!

For larger specimens, use a different approach altogether. Again, lower the water level, but this time until the fish is just covered, and remove all the tank decoration. Using a piece of heavyweight linen, thoroughly soaked in aquarium water, lay it gently over the fish and wrap the fish in it. Next, pick up the fish and transfer it to its transportation container. Be careful, large fish are heavier than you first imagine, and trying to lift them from the bottom of a 60cm(24in) deep aquarium is no easy task. You will probably need help to carry out this task.

Plastic bags are the cheapest way of transporting fish. Use them double and place a layer of newspaper between the two bags. This serves two purposes: it keeps the fish in a relatively dark environment so that it does not get frightened and, should the fin spines penetrate the inner bag, the newspaper should prevent them from puncturing the outer one. The newspaper will also soak up the trickle of water from the punctured bag. Seal the bags with rubber bands and lay the cocooned fish on its side in a polystyrene box to allow the maximum water surface area inside the bag for the fish to 'breathe' during the journey. There only needs to be enough water to cover the fish, so that at least 65 percent of the space is filled with air.

Alternatively, you can transport the fish in buckets with sealable lids, such as those sold for making wine. If you are travelling a long distance, or if the weather is particularly warm, it is a good idea to aerate the water during the journey. To do this, make a hole in the lid to take an airline and attach an airstone to one end and a portable, battery-operated air pump to the other. Always take spare batteries with you in case of delays.

Rinse the filter medium through but keep it damp to ensure that the bacteria survive. You can then replace the filter beds in their containers when you arrive and they will begin to function straight away. If you use as much water from the original installation as possible and ensure that the bacteria are kept alive in the filter medium, you can have the new tank in operation, with the fish installed, in the minimum time.

FILTRATION AND WATER MANAGEMENT

In nature, vital processes of filtration and water management occur naturally, and are aided by the expanse and the flow of the body of water. Changes occur gradually in large bodies of water and water is also constantly being replenished by rain and land drainage. However, in the confines of the 'enclosed ecosystem' of the aquarium, some form of assistance is required to maintain a stable environment and keep the fishes in a healthy condition. Many of the fish diseases and losses most commonly experienced could easily be avoided if fishkeepers paid more attention to water management. This includes installing and maintaining filters, carrying out regular water changes and controlling the water chemistry. In this section, we look at these vital aspects of fishkeeping.

The importance of filtration

In order to keep large fish successfully, it is essential to pay great attention to water management. Without doubt, the question of filtration will loom largely to mind. Indeed, this really deserves prime consideration when planning the design and siting of the aquarium. By necessity, the demands on the filtration system will be great. After all, to accommodate a 'tankbuster' the aquarium will need to be on the large side. This extra volume of water will require considerable turnover in order to be effectively and efficiently treated. Not only does the capacity of the tank require superior filtration, so too does the larger inhabitant; remember that the larger the fish, the greater the demand it places on the filtration system.

How the nitrogen cycle works in the aquarium

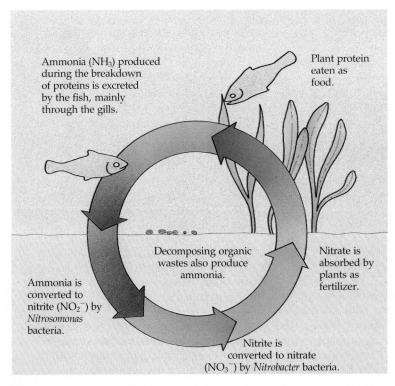

Ammonia (NH$_3$) produced during the breakdown of proteins is excreted by the fish, mainly through the gills.

Plant protein eaten as food.

Decomposing organic wastes also produce ammonia.

Ammonia is converted to nitrite (NO$_2^-$) by *Nitrosomonas* bacteria.

Nitrate is absorbed by plants as fertilizer.

Nitrite is converted to nitrate (NO$_3^-$) by *Nitrobacter* bacteria.

Left: *The aquarium functions as a microcosm of the natural world and, in a well-balanced system, the nitrogen cycle converts ammonia and its byproducts into less harmful and even useful substances. Use regular water changes to reduce nitrate levels.*

Right: *A large canister filter such as this is an excellent way of keeping the aquarium water in good condition. The filter media it holds not only strains out particles from the water but can also perform a useful biological function. This can provide an efficient counterpart to other filtration systems.*

The main purpose of filtration is to artificially aid the natural cycle of converting highly toxic ammonia (NH_3) – primarily produced by the breakdown of proteins and excreted through the gills, but also arising from the decomposition of excreta and other organic material – first into still poisonous nitrites (NO_2^-), and then into less harmful nitrates (NO_3^-). The other main function of the filtration plant is to remove suspended silt and debris, to give the water a 'polished' look. The almost sterile appearance of water in an aquarium is often in stark contrast to the silt-laden or stained waters in which the fishes are found in the wild. Nevertheless, because aquarium water is not constantly replenished, this artificial 'laundering' is essential, not only on aesthetic grounds but also for fundamental biological reasons.

Three main filtration options are available, mechanical, chemical and biological, and these can be used either independently or in conjunction with each other. In fact, some types of filter accomplish all three roles at the same time. Here we examine the options.

A typical large canister filter

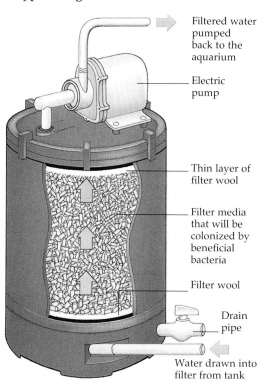

Filtered water pumped back to the aquarium

Electric pump

Thin layer of filter wool

Filter media that will be colonized by beneficial bacteria

Filter wool

Drain pipe

Water drawn into filter from tank

Mechanical filtration

Mechanical filtration simply separates solids from the water as it passes through a suitable filter medium. This process usually involves the water being taken out of the aquarium and treated in a separate container before being returned to the tank. The so-called power filter, a canister fitted with a water pump, is the most common form of this type of mechanical filter. Water is drawn into the bottom of the canister from the aquarium by way of a suction tube, passes through some form of mechanical filtration medium and the pump then drives the water back into the aquarium. The filter medium may take the form of filter wool, coarse nylon matting or hollow cylindrical ceramic pieces. These media also act as a partial biological filter, but are not as effective as the undergravel filter.

Mechanical filters are not cheap, particularly when pumping rates need to turn over the water in the aquarium twice an hour, but when weighed against the value of the fishes and plants being maintained, such cost is not the prime consideration. They also require regular maintenance to remove the trapped particles; the best way of doing this is to replace some of the filter medium every two to three weeks. The reason for replacing only part of the filter medium is that while bacterial action is limited it nonetheless occurs, and retaining a small part of the used medium helps to 'seed' the refreshed filter. It is important to wash any recycled filter medium only in the aquarium water, as changes in temperature or water chemistry could affect the living bacteria. When starting a new power filter installation, use some filter medium from an established power filter to speed the development of efficient water filtration.

Chemical filtration

Chemical filtration refers to any process that alters the chemical composition of the water, and, in a sense, also includes the action of biological filters. The most common chemical filtration media include activated carbon, zeolite, fibrous peat and synthetic ion-exchange resins. Each has a different effect on the water chemistry.

Activated carbon is made from wood, coal

or bone that has been treated at a high temperature in a vacuum to remove the hydrocarbons and then reheated with the addition of oxydizing gases to open millions of pores. Its effect on water is to remove carbon, converting carbon dioxide to oxygen. This is also achieved naturally by plants through photosynthesis, although the process is reversed at night, when oxygen is absorbed and carbon dioxide released. The efficiency of activated carbon depends on the contact time between it and the water. This can be adjusted by altering the speed of water flow through the carbon or by providing a longer or shorter route over which the two are in contact. Not surprisingly, using activated carbon can retard plant growth. If you intend to set up a heavily planted tank – and there is no reason why you should not keep big fish in a planted tank – it is best to consider carefully the use or amount of activated carbon involved. (Protein skimmers will also remove dissolved organic carbon in freshwater systems, even though they are more usually considered – incorrectly – to be useful purely for removing protein waste materials in marine systems.)

Zeolite – a natural mineral substance – is mainly used to remove ammonia from the water. Its use in freshwater systems is somewhat limited, and generally a water change will achieve the same end result. Fibrous peat is one of those substances that will alter the pH value (degree of acidity or alkalinity) of the water. Peat will impart acidity, while crushed shells or coral sand will make the water alkaline. The amounts needed and the pH value required will depend on the natural waters in which the fishes live, and also on the quality of your local water that you use for fishkeeping.

Synthetic ion-exchange resins, which alter the hardness of the water by removing or substituting chemical ions, should be used with great care. Plumbing water softener modules permanently into the filtration plant can lead to excessive demineralization, making the water almost as pure as distilled water. Since this can kill the fish, it is vital to monitor the use of such resins very carefully. The best way of using them is to treat the replacement water when making a partial water change. Here, adding treated water is like the fall of pure rain water into a natural water environment.

Apart from ion-exchange resins, chemical filtration substances are generally used in conjunction with mechanical and biological filters. It is best to place them after the primary filter, acting on the outgoing water flow. Where they are used to alter the fundamental water chemistry, such as pH value or hardness, it is very important to keep a check on the influence they are having and make any necessary adjustments. For this you will need a good water test kit to enable you to diagnose any problems that may occur in the aquarium.

Biological filters
Biological filtration harnesses the power of living bacteria to purify the water in a totally natural way. The various systems simply encourage these bacteria to flourish by providing the right conditions of temperature, oxygen content and water flow, etc. Here we review a range of biological filters and compare their merits.

Undergravel filtration
The simplest, and also the cheapest, form of biological filtration is the undergravel filter. This uses the aquarium substrate – the gravel bed – as the filter medium by suspending it on a perforated plastic plate about 6-10mm above the bottom of the tank. Lift tubes allow the water to be pumped, either by air lift or electric submersible pump, from beneath the gravel bed, causing water to be drawn down through the substrate over the entire tank floor area.

Nitrifying bacteria that naturally grow on the surface of the gravel pieces convert ammonia (NH_3) to nitrites (NO_2^-) and nitrites to nitrates (NO_3^-) as the water passes through. This type of filtration is highly efficient, as long as it is properly installed and maintained. Make sure the filter plate holding the gravel bed clear of the tank bottom is well sealed to the tank sides with aquarium sealant, otherwise water will 'short-circuit' the system. Also, choose the gravel carefully so that it allows free water passage. The best particle size is 0.5-3mm(0.02-0.1in).

Under ideal conditions, this kind of filter can run for several years with just a periodic

A basic undergravel filter plate

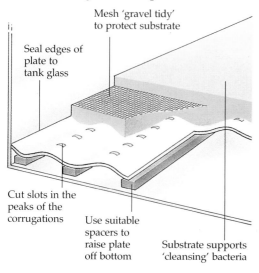

Mesh 'gravel tidy'
to protect substrate

Seal edges of
plate to
tank glass

Cut slots in the
peaks of the
corrugations

Use suitable
spacers to
raise plate
off bottom

Substrate supports
'cleansing' bacteria

Above: *This corrugated plastic sheeting is fine for making a filter plate for undergravel systems and is easy to cut to size to fit large aquariums.*

stirring and cleansing of the gravel. Always do this in the tank, never by removing the gravel, and use water of the same temperature and chemical characteristics. However, there are drawbacks to the undergravel filter system. Since the tank required for your 'tankbuster' will be on the large side, it may be difficult to cover the entire base of the aquarium with filter plates and to seal them properly. Keen 'do-it-yourselfers' can overcome this dilemma by using corrugated plastic panels manufactured for roofing conservatories and outbuildings. Simply trim the panel to the exact plan area of your aquarium and cut drainage slots across the peaks of the corrugations. Position lift tubes at the two rear corners, place suitable piers or spacers between the tank bottom and the panel and then seal the panel to the four walls of the aquarium using silicone sealant.

The easiest form of pumping arrangement is to place an airstone at the bottom of the lift tubes, connected to an air pump. The rising column of bubbles will set up a vertical water flow in the tubes and thus draw water from beneath the filter plates. Alternatively, attach power heads (submersible electric water pumps) to the uplift pipes for more efficient water turnover. Since water flow through the gravel will always follow the path of least resistance, i.e. through the shallowest portion, it is important that the filter bed does not vary greatly in depth. If the water flows through very shallow areas then other deeper regions of gravel will be starved of oxygenated water and the bacteria will die and the efficiency of the system decline.

This problem not only limits the amount and arrangement of aquascaping in a display tank, but also dictates the choice of fish. Many of the Central and South American cichlids, for example, particularly the genus *Cichlasoma* and *Geophagus*, are renowned for their pit-digging habits, and these will clearly impair the efficiency of an undergravel filter. This does not entirely preclude the use of undergravel filters, perhaps with midwater cyprinids such as *Labiobarbus* or the more predatory characin *Hoplias malabaricus*. Plants are also difficult to grow in undergravel filter beds, since they do not benefit from the speedy flow of water past their roots.

Gravity-fed rapid sand filters

The potential efficiency of biological filters can be better achieved by locating the filter bed outside the main aquarium, similar to the arrangement with external power filters. One such option is the so-called gravity-fed rapid sand filter, which is often employed in commercial fish farming establishments and public aquariums. A scaled-down version can be used for single tank operation with amazing results.

It is vital to plan such a setup at a very early stage, as the biological filter is best sited under the main aquarium. Instead of a suction pipe feeding the filter, the aquarium is equipped with an overflow pipe. As water is pumped back into the main aquarium, the level rises to the level of the overflow and falls back into the biological filter tank beneath it. It is most important to install an antisiphonic device in the overflow pipe to ensure that the overflow does not act as a siphon, emptying the main tank and overflowing the biological filter tank. The simplest form of antisiphon system is a small hole (about 1cm/0.4in across) in the overflow pipe above the water level in the aquarium.

The biological filter tank consists of a series of weirs and passages over and under which the water flows. Contained between the weirs are trays of filter media, suspended above the base of the tank in a similar fashion to the undergravel filter described previously. Unlike the aquarium undergravel filter, however, the biological filter tank can successively house different filtration media. For example, the first compartment receiving water directly from the main tank could contain filter wool to trap the larger suspended particles.

The gravity-fed rapid sand filter

Construct this section so that it is easy to replace the wool with fresh supplies depending on the contamination levels in the aquarium. Subsequent compartments can contain filter sand of graded size from coarse to fine. Here, the use of proper filtration sand can be recommended as it is neutral and has no effect on water chemistry. If required, however, you can add media to one or more of the compartments in order to deliberately alter the water chemistry; adding peat will acidify the water, for example, while adding calciferous gravel will harden the water. Place a submersible electric water pump in the final compartment to return the water to the main aquarium. This end compartment can also house the heater-thermostats, away from the damage caused by and to the fish.

Maintenance is similar to that required for undergravel filters in the aquarium, i.e. periodic stirring of the filter beds and the removal of the larger debris and mulm (organic sludge). You can carry out this cleaning process during regular water changes, as it matters little whether the drawn off water comes from the main tank

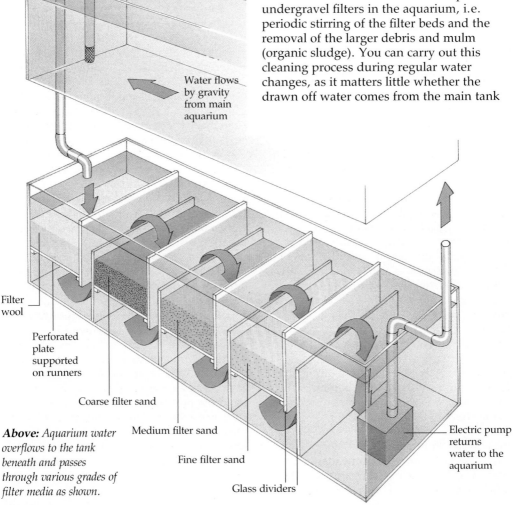

Anti-siphon hole

Water flows by gravity from main aquarium

Filter wool

Perforated plate supported on runners

Coarse filter sand

Medium filter sand

Fine filter sand

Glass dividers

Electric pump returns water to the aquarium

Above: *Aquarium water overflows to the tank beneath and passes through various grades of filter media as shown.*

A basic trickle filter system

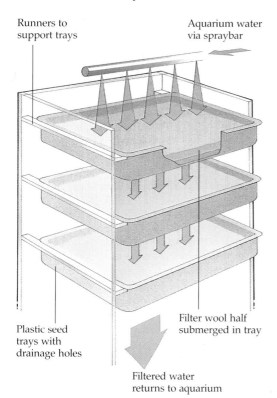

Runners to support trays

Aquarium water via spraybar

Plastic seed trays with drainage holes

Filter wool half submerged in tray

Filtered water returns to aquarium

Above: To maintain two mature filter beds, rotate the top tray to the bottom and recharge with fresh filter wool and move the others up one level.

or the biological filter tank.

A great attraction of this form of filtration is that the total surface area of the system is double that of the aquarium alone, and it is at the surface air/water interface that oxygen exchange takes place. This is important when keeping large fish, as their oxygen demand can be very high, particularly with active specimens. High oxygen levels are also essential to feed the nitrifying bacteria in the biological filter beds.

Trickle filters

Used in conjunction with filters with high flow rates, trickle filters can be very useful as a supplementary method of filtration. Though these filters are better suited to small tanks, especially when raising fry, they do offer a surprisingly efficient method of breaking down nitrites. Water returning from the main filter trickles over a series of

shallow trays, one above the other, each lined with filter wool and containing a layer of filter medium. The water is trickled over the top filter bed by means of a spray bar, and successively passes to the lower beds through apertures in the bottom of each tray. As the water in each tray is very shallow, the filter beds are emersed i.e. partly exposed to the air, and this allows greater oxygen exchange to take place to feed the nitrifying bacteria. Because the water flow is reduced, a trickle filter must be used either as a separate supplementary system to the main filter plant or as a by-pass system to process a small proportion of the returned water from the main filter.

Other filtration options

There are other filters that can be used effectively in water management. Here, we consider two such options: rapid sand filters and diatomaceous earth filters. Pressure-fed rapid sand filters differ from the gravity-fed type in that the filter is an enclosed pressure chamber containing a gravel or sand filter medium. Water is fed under pressure through the sand and returned to the aquarium via a draw-off point at the bottom of the filter. These types of filter are both very expensive and noisy due to the high pressure pumps required to operate them. Their use is better suited to large public aquariums, particularly marine systems, rather than domestic setups.

Diatomaceous earth filters use graded skeletons of diatoms, microscopic organisms with complex skeletal structures, to remove very small particles from the water. Water treated in this way has a high transparency, almost a 'polished' appearance. As the filter is so efficient at removing fine particles it would quickly become blocked if used as the first or only method of filtration. Therefore, it is best used as a post-filter on a gravity-fed rapid sand filter, giving the water a high-quality finish before being returned to the main body of the aquarium. Diatomaceous earth filters need very frequent back-flushing or recharging to retain their efficiency, and since commercially available filters of the size required for large aquariums are few and far between, you should think carefully before installing such a device.

Boosting water flow

With any large tank, water flow may be much less than that experienced by the fish in their natural waters, particularly with riverine species. This natural water flow causes the water at the surface to be constantly changed, allowing oxygen to be absorbed into the water and waste gases such as carbon dioxide to be liberated. To recreate this in the aquarium, it may be necessary to add supplementary water pumps, such as small electric submersible filters, which can often be secreted in a corner of the tank. In large aquariums, their function is not primarily filtration but water agitation and flow, which not only stirs up waterborne sediments, but also turns the water over at the surface to boost oxygen/carbon dioxide exchange.

Making water changes

It is vital to maintain water quality in the aquarium by making regular water changes. No filter, however efficient, will release you from this chore. All aquariums, whatever their size, need regular partial water changes. For example, replacing 10-15 percent of the tank volume every 10-14 days will benefit both fish and plants, and should not be ignored.

It is repeatedly stated in fishkeeping books that the new water must be at the same temperature as the aquarium water. If you are making only a partial water change of 10-15 percent on a frequent basis, however, then cold water trickled in from a hose sprinkler can be very beneficial. After all, even in the tropics the rain is colder than the watercourses on which it falls, and can often prove a trigger for breeding. It does the fish no harm provided the addition is gradual, and it can also lead to healthier and hardier specimens.

Why water chemistry matters

Different fish thrive in different 'water chemistries'. This is because their natural watercourses become tainted with various substances. Forest pools, for example, can easily be affected by the tannins released from the trees both in and around the water, giving the soft water an acidic quality. Conversely, water drainage over limestone rocks will increase the alkalinity and hardness of the water.

The degree of acidity and alkalinity of water is registered by the pH scale, which ranges from 0 (very acid) to 14 (very alkaline), with the midpoint value of 7 denoting neutral. The 'H' of pH represents hydrogen, more specifically the concentration of hydrogen ions (H^+) in the

How the pH scale works

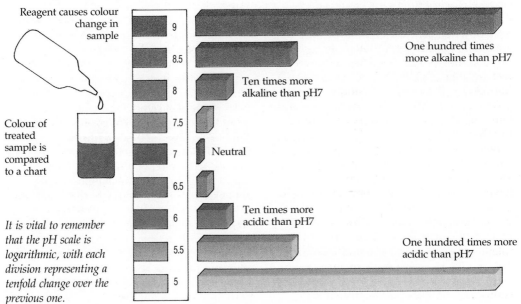

Reagent causes colour change in sample

Colour of treated sample is compared to a chart

It is vital to remember that the pH scale is logarithmic, with each division representing a tenfold change over the previous one.

9
8.5
8
7.5
7   Neutral
6.5
6
5.5
5

One hundred times more alkaline than pH7

Ten times more alkaline than pH7

Ten times more acidic than pH7

One hundred times more acidic than pH7

Above: *Water quality in*   *underlying rocks and*
rivers and lakes depends   *runoff from the*
on many factors, such as   *surrounding land.*

water. It is the hydrogen ions that cause acidity and the hydroxyl ions (OH⁻), the other ionized component of the water molecule (H_2O), that cause alkalinity. Thus, the pH scale reflects the relative concentration of hydrogen ions and hydroxyl ions in any solution. Just to complicate matters, the pH scale is not linear but logarithmic and reflects hydrogen ion concentration in inverse proportion. The logarithmic scale means that a jump of one unit represents a ten-fold change in hydrogen ion concentration (two units a hundred-fold change, etc.) and inverse proportion means that the more hydrogen ions present in the water the lower the number on the scale.

Being a logarithmic scale, a seemingly small shift in pH value can have a critical effect on the fish. Many freshwater fish have a relatively broad tolerance range, but even this rarely extends much beyond pH values of 6.5-8.5. Some freshwater fish have more defined limits, while others will tolerate unsuitable water conditions but will not attempt breeding or enjoy longevity.

Water hardness, another very important component of water chemistry, is a reflection of the dissolved salt content. By far the majority of dissolved substances in water consist of four negatively charged ions: chlorides (Cl⁻), sulphates (SO_4^{--}), carbonates (CO_3^{--}) and bicarbonates (HCO_3^-); and positively charged ions: calcium (Ca^{++}), magnesium (Mg^{++}), sodium (Na^+) and potassium (K^+). There are various scales to register water hardness, the most widely used in fishkeeping circles being °dH and mg/litre $CaCO_3$. For example, very soft water registers as 3°dH (0-50mg/litre $CaCO_3$) and very hard water as over 25°dH (over 450mg/litre $CaCO_3$). As with pH value, water hardness varies between different locations. Stretches of the Rio Negro in South America, for example, contain very soft water, down to 3°dH, whereas some African Rift Valley Lakes contain hard water that registers 18-22°dH.

Where fish require soft water, add a proportion of well-filtered rain water during a water change. To make the water harder, add normal tap water (usually hard) to the aquarium. Alternatively, use calciferous rocks, such as limestone, in the filter or as a tank decoration.

Test kits are widely available for checking pH value, hardness, and levels of ammonia, nitrite and nitrate in the water. Use them sensibly – they are especially important when setting up a new aquarium, for example – but do not become paranoid over their use and the adjustment of water conditions. With experience, you should be able to tell the state of your tank by the condition and reactions of the fish and plants. Then test kits become like a first-aid kit – available for emergencies.

Water temperature
Water temperature is just as important as water chemistry. Invariably, tropical fish are kept at too high a temperature, where slightly cooler conditions would be more beneficial. Increasing the temperature decreases the amount of dissolved oxygen, and the larger the fish, the greater the oxygen demand. Provided you avoid extremes, the lower the temperature the more active and long-lived your fish will be. Where a temperature range is given for a particular fish, keep to the lower levels. See individual species entries for more details.

AQUASCAPING

Aquascaping is a matter of personal preference. More importantly, it must suit the fish that live in the environment you create for them. This must be your prime consideration. For example, tinfoil barbs (*Barbus schwanenfeldi*) are active, midwater fishes that need a bright spacious aquarium with plenty of open water for swimming, and their liking for liberal amounts of vegetable matter in their diet will certainly dictate your choice of plants. On the other hand, a predatory shovelnosed catfish (*Sorubim lima*) will be perfectly happy in relatively gloomy surroundings with overhanging branches and thickets of plants in which to lurk in wait for prey.

Once you have determined the needs of your fishes, you can then choose the materials for decorating the tank and arrange them to form the ideal aquascape for all concerned. Here we look at the aspects you need to consider.

Above: *A shovelnose catfish* (Sorubim lima) *at home in a dimly lit aquarium that offers plenty of hiding places and resting stations. This is a good example of aquascaping that not only suits the fish but also allows the aquarist plenty of opportunities for creative design.*

Left: *This is quite a contrast to the above tank. Here, a brightly lit aquarium plays host to deep-bodied shoaling fish* (Semaprochilodus taeniurus) *that relish the generous swimming room offered by their spacious and uncluttered surroundings. Such fish also need a good flow of water in the aquarium.*

Aquarium background

The most commonly available backgrounds are the rolls of plastic backing sold by length in aquarium shops. These come in a variety of designs and although they may be cut to any length, the standard heights are only 30cm(12in) and 45cm(18in), making them unsuitable for deeper aquariums. However, if you find a suitable design and size of backing then attach it to the outside of the aquarium using double-sided tape.

Painting the external surface of the back pane of the aquarium black is an effective starting point. This gives a good impression of depth once the aquarium is filled with water and the rocks, wood and plants added. Alternatively, apply a layer of the adhesive plastic sold for covering table tops. This is available in a choice of plain colours and the limited widths can be joined to cover the whole of the back of the tank. Ensure that there are no traces of dirt or grease on the surface of the glass and take great care to avoid trapping any air bubbles when you apply the plastic sheeting, or the overall effect will be spoilt.

For a completely different approach to aquarium backgrounds, try using unvarnished cork tiles. Stick these to the back and side inner walls of the tank with silicone sealant before adding the water. Again, ensure that the glass is clean and free from grease and attach the tiles so that there are no gaps between them and the glass in which fishes, uneaten food or waste material can become trapped. You can choose from a variety of surface textures on the tiles. Avoid buying those with hardboard backing because the adhesive used to attach the cork to the hardboard may be harmful to fish. One of the main advantages of using cork tiles becomes apparent when planting the aquarium, as they form an excellent surface for anchoring such plants as Java fern and Java moss.

In the same way, you can attach thin sheets of slate to the back of the aquarium with silicone sealant, or perhaps small pieces of rock to create a rocky shore setting. This is not advisable if you are keeping easily frightened fishes, as they may be injured by dashing against the rocks, dislodging scales or, worse still, cutting themselves in the process.

Choosing the ideal substrate

Talk about substrates and the most usual item mentioned is gravel. Natural aquarium gravel is brown/grey in colour, with rounded pebbles 3-8mm(0.1-0.3in) in diameter, depending on the grade. It is available in convenient quantities from most aquatic stores. When calculating the amount required for the aquarium, bear in mind that 6kg(just over 13lb) of gravel will cover 900cm^2(144in^2), i.e. a base area measuring 30cm by 30cm(12in x 12in) to a depth of approximately 2.5cm(1in). An overall depth of 5cm(2in) should be sufficient for most fishes. Check that the gravel is lime-free if you are intending to keep softwater fishes. Sometimes, gravel is collected from gravel pits or offshore sites where quantities of shell become mixed with it. This shell slowly dissolves, releasing calcium and hardening the water. The only drawback with gravel is that it is somewhat coarse for those fish that like to bury themselves or that feed by filtering the substrate.

Filtration sand provides a fine alternative to gravel. This is a totally inert, honey-coloured, non-compacting sand that allows water to pass freely through it. It is available from swimming pool suppliers, but check that you have the correct grit size – the coarse grade has a particle size of 3mm(0.1in) and the fine grade a particle size down to 0.5mm(0.02in). Filtration sand provides an excellent substrate for fishes such as *Pseudohemiodon laticeps*, a whiptail catfish that likes to bury itself in the sand until only its eyes are visible, or *Pseudodoras niger*, one of the talking catfishes that feeds by filtering sand through its mouth and out through the gills; with coarser gravels, the delicate gill rakers may become damaged. When calculating your requirements, allow approximately 50 percent more sand than gravel for the same area of aquarium floor.

Other possible substrates include lava rock, an inert reddish material ideal for cichlid aquariums, and a scree made by crushing slate. Although the latter is a time-consuming job, the finished effect is well worth the effort involved.

Whichever substrate you decide to use, always wash it thoroughly to remove all dust before placing it in the aquarium. With community tanks of smaller fishes it is

AQUASCAPING OPTIONS IN THE AQUARIUM
Backgrounds

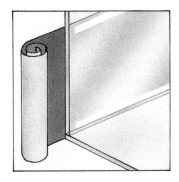

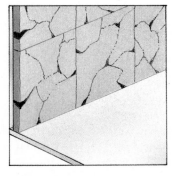

Plastic backing – plain or with a suitable design – can be taped or stuck to the outside of the tank.

Textured cork tiles fixed on the inside with silicone sealant are excellent for attaching plants.

Also consider using sheets of slate stuck with silicone sealant, but avoid leaving sharp edges.

Rocks

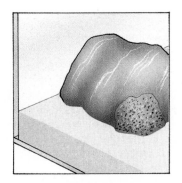

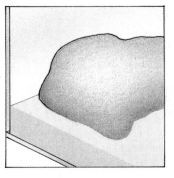

Granite and other completely inert rocks will not affect the water chemistry in the aquarium.

Limestone and other calciferous rocks will make the water harder - make sure they are suitable.

Pieces of slate are ideal for making terraces and caves that fish will use as hiding places.

Plants attached to wood or rocks

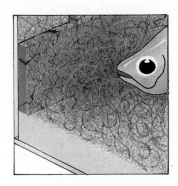

Hardy Java fern (Microsorium pteropus) *attached to wood and rocks will thrive in all tanks.*

African water fern (Bolbitis heudelotii) *wired to a support will flourish near a spraybar.*

Prolific Java moss (Vesicularia dubyana) *grows well and is an ideal forage for plant-eating fishes.*

Substrates

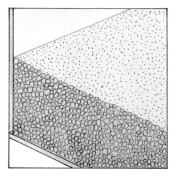

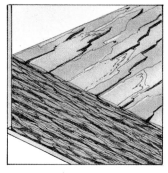

Fine sand with rounded grains is ideal for fishes that like to bury themselves in the substrate.

Standard aquarium gravel is a good all-purpose substrate. Add shell fragments for harder water.

A coarse scree of slate fragments makes a novel tank substrate that will suit the robust fishes.

Wood and its substitutes

Good pieces of bogwood are expensive but make excellent features for fish and viewers.

Vine roots offer a lighter, more textured look that creates a very decorative effect in the aquarium.

Pieces of synthetic wood can look very convincing and are ideal for hiding items of tank hardware.

Normally rooted plants and their substitutes

Amazon sword plants can be planted in baskets and the base protected with a layer of rocks.

Cryptocoryne species, here shown planted in the substrate, provide a wide choice of elegant shapes.

Plastic plants may be the only option for destructive fishes, but they can look very acceptable.

usually recommended that the substrate is sloped from the rear of the tank down towards the front. However, many large fishes tend to perform their own aquascaping and move the substrate to suit themselves, either using their mouths or inadvertantly banking the sand or gravel with sudden, and powerful, flicks of their caudal fins.

Above: *The large rocks in this aquarium create an effective underwater landscape. Build them up in stable arrangements to avoid dangerous falls.*

Using rocks in the aquarium

The choice of rock is a matter of individual preference. Among the most suitable for the aquarium are the igneous rocks, such as granite, basalt and gneiss. Garden centres offer larger pieces of granite for rockeries and are a good source of supply; aquarium shops normally have smaller pieces for sale. Slate is also popular. It is a metamorphic rock, i.e. the original clay rock has undergone considerable changes through heat and pressure to yield blue-grey rock that splits easily along well-defined cleavage planes. It is very versatile in the aquarium; thin slabs can be used as cave roofs or small sections glued together with silicone sealant to create terraces. The main disadvantage of

slate is the potential hazard caused by the sharp edges where the rock fractures. All these rocks are inert; they will not leach any potentially harmful substances, such as lime, copper or lead, into the water.

Most sedimentary rocks, such as limestone, chalk and some calciferous sandstones (i.e. those in which the sand grains are cemented together with limestone), should be avoided as the calcium leaches slowly into the water and hardens it. Do not use them in soft water, unless you deliberately want to harden the water to keep hardwater fishes in a softwater area. In this case, it would be better to use the rocks in the filtration system where you can control the amounts used and thus regulate the degree of hardness. A tried and tested method of judging whether a rock or sample of gravel contains calcium or magnesium compounds liable to harden the water is to pour some vinegar (acetic acid), or a few drops of hydrochloric or sulphuric acid on it. If the rock effervesces, discard it; if there is no reaction, it should be safe to use, but it is wise to test it in a tank of water before putting it in the main aquarium.

Before using any rocks, wash them to remove any mud, moss or algae, a job best done outside using a hosepipe. When placing them in the aquarium, always seat them on the base glass. This will avoid them being dislodged by the fishes and fracturing the aquarium glass. And remember that in large aquariums the rocks will be equally large in proportion, and so you may need help to manhandle them into position.

Wood for that natural look
Bogwood is a familiar sight in aquarium shops. Notoriously expensive to buy, it is well worth taking time over choosing the best pieces. At all costs avoid any that have been sawn; the unnatural straight edges are extremely difficult to camouflage. Before using bogwood in the aquarium, brush off any dust and loose splinters and soak the pieces for several days, changing the water

Below: A well-marked piece of wood provides a perfect foil and resting place for this specimen of Pterygoplichthys gibbiceps - *a catfish.*

each day. Then position the bogwood in the aquarium, taking care to seat heavy pieces directly on the base glass rather than precariously on the substrate. Occasionally, you may buy a piece of wood that floats. In this case, fix it to a plate of glass or a piece of slate with silicone sealant and anchor this securely in the substrate.

Vine roots are an interesting alternative to bogwood. Probably the best place to find vine roots is in a florist. They are popular for floral arrangements and when you see their delicate texture you will wonder why they are not equally popular for tank decoration. They are much lighter in both colour and weight then bogwood, and need exactly the same treatment before use.

Synthetic wood is now available but only as relatively small pieces, the largest being about 50cm(20in). Although several, perhaps identical, pieces would need to be joined together to make an impact in a large aquarium, a little artistic flair and the careful use of plants should produce a pleasing aquascape using these materials.

Using plants effectively
Plants help to provide a stable system in the aquarium, acting as a buffer against rapid increases in nitrite levels, fluctuating pH levels and sudden bacterial blooms. It is possible to establish plants with large fish, but you need patience – especially when it sometimes takes a while for the fish to arrive at the same conclusion!

Perhaps the easiest plant to establish in the aquarium is Java fern (*Microsorium pteropus*). It is tolerant of most water conditions, growing longer, darker green leaves in hard water and shorter, paler leaves in soft water. Do not plant it in the substrate but attach it to the wood, rocks or even the cork background using green garden wire or fishing line. Eventually, it will root onto the wood or rock and spread. It multiplies by growing small plantlets along the leaf margins. When these are large enough to handle, you can detach them and fix them to a suitable surface. Conveniently, all types of fish seem to leave this plant in place; even plant-eaters leave it alone. It is also a shade-tolerant plant, thriving particularly well in the darker areas of the aquarium.

Another aquatic fern that can be grown in the same manner as Java fern is *Bolbitis heudelotii*. It is slightly more demanding than Java fern, flourishing in clear, soft to medium-hard water and at higher light levels. It seems to thrive especially well beneath the spraybar return from a power filter. Again, do not plant this species in the aquarium substrate.

Java moss (*Vesicularia dubyana*) is a common site in many furnished aquariums. It will attach itself to rocks and wood and soon carpets the area with lush, green growth. Problems occur when this plant becomes too prolific and it is vital to remove the excess growth regularly. Uneaten food particles and faeces may become trapped within the moss and the best way of removing this debris is to flush water through the plants during regular water changes. It is a very useful plant in the

Below: The dark green fronds of an African water fern (Bolbitis   heudelotti) *glint in the aquarium lights. A fine plant for clean water.*

aquarium if you are keeping plant-eating fishes; its rapid growth rate enables fishes to continually graze it with no ill-effects to either fish or plant.

Among the most well-known specimen plants for the aquarium are the various species of *Echinodorus*, the Amazon sword plants. There are more than 50 species, and the genus as a whole covers a wide range, from tropical South America to the southern United States. Most species are marsh plants and are found growing on river banks and in swampy areas liable to flooding. During high water, the plants adapt by growing underwater leaves that are often quite different from their emerse (above water) growth. The plants offered for sale in shops have usually been grown in their emerse form, either in specialist aquatic plant nurseries using mist spray techniques or in Asian plant nurseries operated as a secondary business to fish farming. (Waste water from the fish farms is high in nitrites and other waste products and makes an excellent liquid fertilizer for growing plants.)

Amazon swords are tolerant of most water conditions as long as extremes of hardness and pH are avoided. Normal aquarium temperatures of 20-25°C(68-77°F) are fine. They require a sandy substrate and may benefit from the addition of nutrients in the form of clay pellets at the roots. Insert the young plants into the growing medium so that the crown is level with the substrate, otherwise they are prone to rotting. Initially, the leaves will die back and the plant will appear dead, but do not panic! Small leaf shoots will appear from the basal crown and eventually develop into a beautiful rosette of leaves. This process of planting, die back, root development and eventual leaf growth may take several weeks, so be patient.

To accompany fishes that are persistent diggers, it may be better to plant Amazon swords in pond baskets. Line the basket with hessian and growing medium and insert the plants as described above. You can establish the planted basket in the main aquarium or grow it on in another tank, transferring it to the display aquarium when it is fully established. Hide the basket behind rocks or wood and add a few

undulating leaf margins that make it a very attractive specimen plant for the large aquarium. However, it is well worth trying any species that become available.

Various species of *Cryptocoryne* are also worth including in the aquarium. Plant these in the same way as Amazon swords. Their emerse leaves will quickly rot off and should be removed to prevent the rot spreading to the crown of the plant. It will take up to two months for the plant to establish a root system and begin to produce leaves. Most *Cryptocoryne* species are slow-growing and are more demanding in their temperature requirements and water conditions than Amazon swords but will reward patience and perseverance by putting on a good show in the aquarium. Species are often difficult to distinguish unless the plant is in flower, but they are now available as named plants from aquatic shops and centres. Recommended species include *Cryptocoryne affinis*, a hardy plant tolerant of lower temperatures and suitable for both the coldwater and tropical aquariums, and *Cryptocoryne balansae*, an elegant plant with long (40cm/16in plus), narrow, bright green leaves covered with small indentations. Once established, *C. balansae* propagates readily by runners and soon forms a dense thicket that may require regular thinning to prevent the individual plants deteriorating. It does not like large water changes. Also recommended are *Cryptocoryne ciliata*, which prefers harder water and will grow to 40cm or more, but is sometimes difficult to establish and benefits from the addition of clay pellets to the roots, and *Cryptocoryne usteriana* (*C. aponogetafolia*), which, although rarely offered for sale, is a magnificent plant for the large aquarium. It is difficult to establish and prefers moderately acid water, but once established will produce straplike leaves up to 60cm(24in) long, covered with rows of blisterlike dimples.

Above: *A flourishing Java fern (Microsorium pteropus). Attach this undemanding and sturdy plant to wood or rocks in the display aquarium.*

strategically placed large stones to prevent the fish from removing the plant from the basket. Using baskets has several advantages over permanent planting: excessive growth can be checked by trimming the roots as they emerge from the basket; the tank decor can be changed easily by growing suitable replacement plants in another aquarium; and any damaged plants can be removed and allowed to recover in a spare tank while substitutes occupy their places in the show aquarium.

Among the most successful Amazon swords for larger aquariums are: *Echinodorus bleheri* (*E. paniculatus*), a mature plant having about 20-25 leaves up to 35cm(14in) long; *Echinodorus cordifolius*, a species that will tolerate much cooler conditions (down to 10°C/50°F) and is suitable for the coldwater aquarium; *Echinodorus horizontalis*, a species that thrives in clear, soft water at a relatively higher temperature range of 25-27°C(77-81°F); and *Echinodorus major*, the so-called ruffled Amazon sword, which has

Should you decide that live plants are really not for you, then there is a wide range of plastic plants available, and it is possible to achieve some striking displays with care. Perhaps the ideal strategy is to use plastic plants as feature plants and combine them with live Java moss and Java fern, thus gaining the best of both worlds.

FEEDING

Fishes need a varied diet for good health. In the wild, they can forage or hunt for items most suited to their needs, but in the aquarium, they are dependent on the hand that feeds them. Examination of stomach contents of wild-caught fishes shows that they gain nourishment from unexpected sources. Some so-called vegetarians, such as many of the loricariid catfishes, are found to consume small crustaceans as well as algae, and the predatory pimelodid, *Phractocephalus hemioliopterus*, has been known to consume the fruits of trees growing alongside the rivers. In fact, many wild fishes feed on terrestrial insects, flowers, fruits and seeds of trees, as well as on aquatic plants and animals. With this in mind, it is clearly beneficial to offer as wide a range of foods as possible to your fishes.

How much and how often?
A problem encountered by all aquarists is how often to feed the fish. In general community tanks, this is quite simple – a pinch of flake food sufficient for the fish to consume within five to ten minutes. This, with the occasional offering of live *Daphnia*,

given once or maybe twice a day, will keep your fish fit and healthy.

Temperature will affect the amount of food consumed by your fish. Each fish has an optimum temperature range. If the temperature drops close to or below the lower end of this range the fish will refuse to feed. In the same way, goldfish kept in a garden pond stop feeding during the autumn and do not start again until the water temperature begins to rise in the spring. Higher temperatures speed up the fishes metabolism and they may be expected to consume more, but this is not necessarily the case. When the water temperature exceeds their normal range, the fish become stressed and one of the ways this becomes apparent is loss of appetite.

To feed larger fish correctly it is necessary to understand the habits of the fish in the wild. Predatory species, for example, are used to hunting for their food; they may eat well one day but not at all for the next

Below: A tame redtailed catfish takes food from the hand, but resist the temptation to overfeed this predatory species – it needs periods of fasting.

three, and it is this system of eating and fasting that should be maintained in the aquarium. Try feeding predators about three times a week. At each feed, provide sufficient food to give them a distended belly and do not feed them again until they have digested this meal, shown by the stomach returning to its normal shape. Digestion time varies with the type of foods: prawn and fish are digested quickest, followed by commercial tablet foods, and lastly, high-protein strips of meat, such as beef heart or fly larvae (maggots).

When a fish is sated, it will normally refuse further offerings and retire to a quiet corner to digest its meal. However, some fish break all the rules. Some cichlids and catfish will gorge themselves seven days a week if the opportunity presents itself. This may produce a rapid growth rate, but it does little for the health of the fish. In an aquarium, fishes are not able to exercise as much as they would in the wild, and therefore they are unable to burn off these excesses. They build up in the body and result in an overweight and unhealthy specimen. This can be partially alleviated by ensuring that there is good water flow from the filtration system, which will encourage the fish to swim against it and thereby exercise itself.

Omnivores will eat anything and everything, from shrimps and pieces of fish to commercial foods and plant material. These are the easiest to feed and can be fed each day, but again take care not to overfeed them.

Vegetarians are more of a problem. The very nature of their food means that they need to consume relatively large amounts to extract sufficient nutrients. Feeding on plants is a very inefficient way of gaining nourishment, and vegetarian fishes continually browse, in much the same way as cows and sheep. The plant material is broken down in the gut and the nutrients extracted. However, a large amount of nutrients pass out in the faeces and these provide excellent food for the plants in the aquarium. So high in nutrient can these faeces be, in fact, that some fishes – the catfish *Pseudodoras niger*, for example – have adapted to include these waste products from herbivores within their diet.

Coping with holidays

Holidays are always a problem. It is best to leave all fishes unfed during this period, and no harm will come to them for up to two weeks. However, it is wise to get a neighbour, or better still a fellow hobbyist, to come in and check that the filtration and heating systems are working; the lighting can be left on a time switch. If you leave a neighbour in charge, make sure they have the telephone number of a reliable and knowledgeable friend who is willing to visit at short notice, should an emergency arise. On no account leave a novice in charge of feeding as the results can be disastrous – fishes overfed, an accumulation of uneaten food putting a strain on the filtration system, polluted water, etc.

During this time, the predators will just think that food is in short supply, the omnivores will eat any bits and pieces that have accumulated in the aquarium, and the herbivores will graze on the plants – a very good reason for having real plants in the aquarium. Although this will knock back the plants in the short term, they will soon recover when you return and resume the normal feeding regime. When you do start feeding again after a break, resist the temptation to overfeed by building up to normal feeding levels gradually.

Choosing the most suitable foods

The aquarist market today is full of good, nutritious offerings, from freeze-dried worms and fly larvae, to frozen shrimps, mussels and fish, which can be combined with the standard tablet and flake foods. In addition, you can buy fresh fish and crustaceans from your local fishmonger or supermarket. A visit to the food store will provide lettuce, spinach, peas and a variety of fruits that can also be a useful source of nourishment for your fishes.

Very often, newly imported predatory fishes, especially more mature specimens, will refuse to feed. There are two options open to you: continue offering dead foods and hope that the fish will take them or offer live fish. Only the aquarist can come to terms with his or her own conscience in dealing with this problem. The ethics are simple – do you feed the predatory fish its natural diet of live fish or allow it, instead of the prey, to die? If you cannot come to terms with this fact of life, then perhaps you should reconsider your choice of fish.

The normal live foods, such as *Daphnia*, *Tubifex* worms and river shrimps (*Palaemonetes varians*) may be too small for predatory fish to bother about and the only other option is to provide food fish. Often, it is only necessary to feed live fish during the acclimatization period, and once your predator has started to feed, has put on weight and is looking healthy, it may be possible to wean it onto dead meat. You can buy food fish from your local aquatic dealer, breed them at home or catch them in unpolluted local rivers and ponds. A word of caution if you are intending to catch your own live food: results of work carried out at Blijdorp Zoo in Rotterdam showed that the lethal accumulations of PCBs (polychlorbiphenyls) that had built up in the body fats of *Arapaima gigas* were probably due to the high levels of PCBs in fodder fish. These had been caught in western Holland in the lower reaches of the heavily polluted Rhine. It is also important to watch out for infestations of fish lice, anchor worm and other parasites and infections in wild-caught fish and to avoid introducing these into the aquarium.

It is possible to encourage predatory fishes to take dead foods. Using a needle and cotton, thread a piece of fish or prawn (with the shell still on) onto the cotton and, holding one end, dangle the morsel in the aquarium. As it drifts with the current, jerk it gently once or twice so that it moves against the flow. If the predator is hungry enough it will take the food before it realizes that it is dead. Most predators wait to see a food item move before lunging at it, and if this can be simulated, the battle is won. Once your fish realizes what an easy meal is, it will continue to feed without hesitation. Do make sure that there is no knot or loop at the end of the cotton to prevent the food from slipping off easily.

Smaller live foods, such as *Daphnia*, *Tubifex*, mosquito larvae, bloodworms and whiteworms, etc., are suitable for many of the midwater fishes and also for the bottom-dwelling filter feeders, but you will need copious amounts for a large shoal of barbs or for a large catfish such as *Pseudodoras*

niger. Although small and seemingly useless for most large fishes, *Daphnia* are ideal for feeding large filter feeders such as the paddlefish, *Polyodon spathula*. *Daphnia*, mosquito larvae and bloodworms (midge larvae) can be collected from local ponds. Ensure that these ponds do not contain fishes, that the water is clear and sweet smelling, surrounded with deciduous trees and with a layer of leaf litter on the bottom. Where ponds are seasonal and dry up during the summer months, try culturing *Daphnia*, bloodworms, gnat larvae and other suitable live foods in a clean water butt.

In collecting live food you will undoubtedly gather several 'unwanted' creatures at the same time. Those might include such creatures as damselfly and dragonfly larvae or the larvae of the great diving beetle, *Dytiscus marginalis*. If you have no use for these animals, please return them to the pond. If you do want to use them as food then you can offer them to anything with a mouth large enough to eat them, but do ensure that they are all consumed by the fish. All three larvae have good sets of jaws and, if left unnoticed or uneaten in the aquarium, they will inflict wounds on even the largest fish. These wounds are then open to secondary infections from fungi and bacteria. Dragonflies, damselfishes and water beetles all fly, and can be visitors to your garden ponds so, if you use your pond as a source of food you will need to exercise the same amount of care in checking what you are putting into your aquarium.

Live river shrimp are welcomed by most fishes. The high calcium content of their shells is also beneficial to growing fish. You should be able to buy these from your local aquatic dealer but they may not be available during times of adverse weather.

There are a number of live foods that are usually considered to be for amphibians and reptiles rather than for fishes, but reports of studies of stomach contents in the field suggest that there is no reason why we should not offer them to our fish. Crickets and mealworms make excellent foods, for example, the only disadvantage is that the crickets tend to escape very easily and can be extremely aggravating when chirping noisily in the lounge.

The fishing tackle shop offers fly larvae (maggots). These can be kept in the fridge until needed as food. Feed sparingly, and check that the fish are digesting them. Some species, such as the South American lungfish, *Lepidosiren paradoxa*, although consuming the maggots avidly, seem unable to digest them and the maggots pass straight through the gut and appear in a gelatinous coating of mucus among the faeces. The African lungfish, *Protopterus annectens*, on the other hand, greedily eats maggots and digests them with ease. Earthworms are easy to obtain and are eagerly consumed by most fishes, although some catfishes seem to take fright if the worm wriggles rapidly near their barbels. To construct a simple worm trap, place a piece of hessian sacking in the garden and cover it with a layer of tea leaves. Worms will make their way to this and, if the layer of tea leaves is thick enough to exclude the frost, you will be able to lift the corner of the hessian and collect clean worms, even during the harshest weather conditions. Before the hessian decomposes, either start

Below: Some fish are simplicity to feed. This S. American characin, Semaprochilodus taeniurus, *will readily take peas in its diet.*

a new patch or place another piece of hessian on top of the first and continue with your existing patch.

Some fish, such as the catfish, *Megalodoras irwini*, are specialized feeders. In the wild, *Megalodoras* feeds on snails. You can grow these in a garden pond or in another aquarium and use them to supplement the fish's diet. Many other fish, such as cichlids, will also take snails, although these may have to be crushed before being put into the tank. *Ampularia* snails (apple snails) breed very easily and are a good source of food. Malaysian burrowing snails (*Melanoides* sp.) are not acceptable to most fishes, as the tight spiral of their shells prevents the fish from crushing them.

Frozen foods are excellent, being easy to store and free from disease. They are available in handy packets and convenient to use – simply break off chunks as you need them. For the smaller foods, allow the frozen lump to dissolve in the aquarium, but it is best to thaw larger items, such as sand eels, before feeding them to the fish. As an alternative, buy frozen blocks of prawn and whitebait from the fishmonger and, for those fish that can cope, fresh small trout and sprats may be fed whole.

Beef heart is a particularly nutritious meaty food. Remove the fat and slice the heart into suitably sized pieces before use. Alternatively, ask your butcher to mince the heart for you and store it in the freezer for use as needed. Always feed beef heart sparingly; an excess can easily result in overweight fishes.

For plant eaters, the most common items are lettuce and peas, but this is only the start. Small tomatoes, figs, pieces of pear and banana, grapes, brussel sprouts and pieces of carrot are all worth trying. Make sure that the fruit is fairly ripe, as it would be when it falls from the trees in the wild. It may be necessary to scald the harder green leaves of lettuce and cabbage to break down the outer cell walls and make them easier to eat, or crush them in your hand to break the outer cellulose layer. If possible, grow your own green foods so that you know what has gone into or onto them; it is always possible that your fish may be affected by pesticides and other chemicals on shop-bought vegetables and fruit.

BASIC HEALTH CARE

Most of the common diseases occur when fish are kept in less than ideal conditions. They may be overcrowded, the diet may be incorrect, fighting and bullying may occur, or water conditions could be at fault. Under normal circumstances, the bacteria that live on and within fish remain low in number and do no harm. Viruses and fungal spores are also present within the closed system of the aquarium. Just as healthy humans are normally able to resist viral and bacterial infections, so can healthy fishes. Should they become weakened in some way, however, perhaps through transportation, overcrowding or poor aquarium conditions, they will sicken and, if a suitable treatment or a change in conditions are not applied fairly quickly, may die.

The key to a happy, healthy fish lies not only in good aquarium management but also in the provision of the correct diet. Even the lack of some vitamins can cause illness. The lack of Vitamin A, for example, can cause loss of appetite, eye and gill problems and haemorrhaging at the base of the fins.

Once established in the aquarium, fishes rarely suffer from many diseases. The most common complaints are ripped fins as a result of fighting, dislodged scales, cuts and abrasions from jumping or dashing against unsuitable tank decorations or as a result of mishandling. In well-maintained systems, these complaints will normally heal without any intervention from the aquarist. However, if there are strains on the system, such as overcrowding or inefficient filtration, secondary infections from bacteria or fungal spores may set in.

Often, the fishes show warning signs of any impending deterioration in water conditions. Check the fish every day for any signs of degeneration of the membrane between the fins rays, for the disintegration of barbels or sloughing of the body mucus. These are all clear signs that things are beginning to go wrong. In most cases, making a water change and checking to see that the filtration system is working efficiently are usually all that is required to rectify the situation. Where regular maintenance is carried out, these symptoms rarely arise.

The major problems of disease occur on newly imported fish. In fact, some fish carry a very clear legacy from their wild habitat in the shape of external parasites. Over the last few years, there have been instances of fish imported from South America with a large parasite attached to them, usually on the head. This creature is almost transparent and attaches itself to its host with hooked feet. Once attached, it rasps at the surface of the host. The easiest method of removal is by using tweezers and gently pulling the creature from the fish. Take care to guard against infection of the attachment wound. So far, this particular parasite has defied attempts to identify it.

Even if they are not playing host to a large parasite, newly imported fish are vulnerable because they have been subjected to the rigours of transportation and the associated delays at airports while they clear customs. Before shipment, food will normally have been withheld so that they do not foul the water in their transportation bags. Sometimes antibiotics and other medications are added to the water in which they are to be carried. Nevertheless, the fish still suffer shock and, if mishandled at their destination, will fall prey to bacterial and viral infections. Reputable wholesalers and retailers are equipped to cope with this and are able to deal with any outbreaks of disease, so that predominantly healthy fishes are offered for sale to the general public.

Although it is advisable to have a small supply of medications available to cover the more common ailments, do remember that they have a limited shelf life and should be checked for viability at regular intervals. Some substances also need to be kept in dark or cool conditions. Wherever they are stored, ensure that they are kept out of reach of animals and children. Ideally, buy a comprehensive guide to fish diseases that you can understand and acquaint yourself with your local veterinarian and any associated aquatic advisors. It is also wise to have a range of spares for the aquarium 'life-support' systems, such as replacement bearings, 'O' seals, diaphragms, heaters and thermostats, in case of breakdown. These systems are literally your fish's lifeline.

Before we briefly consider a range of common diseases and parasites, it is worth repeating that regular maintenance,

prevention of overcrowding and careful feeding and handling will greatly enhance the health and well-being of all the fishes in your care.

FINROT

This is characterized by white edges on affected fins and degeneration of the fin membrane and rays. The condition is caused by bacteria, such as *Aeromonas*. Finrot usually occurs on fish that have been subjected to mishandling during transportation or overcrowding in the aquarium, reducing their disease resistance to a low ebb.

If caught at an early stage, finrot is easy to tackle with a proprietary antibacterial treatment and by improving the environmental conditions for the affected fish. More persistent cases may need the use of antibiotics such as chlortetracycline or oxytetracycline hydrochloride, both administered as a bath for up to five days, at a dosage rate of 10-20mg/litre for chlortetracycline and 20-100mg/litre for oxytetracycline hydrochloride. This treatment may need repeating. Depending on where you live, you may need to obtain these antibiotics from your veterinarian. In any event, always seek expert advice if you are at all unsure about using such remedies.

Above: *Although quite attractive, this is a parasite often found on fish imported from South America. It clings tenaciously to its host, usually on the head. Remove it carefully and treat the wound against secondary infection.*

Right: *Finrot on a tail. Bacterial infections such as this are liable to set in when the fins have become damaged. If left untreated, the infection can spread to the body. Improving conditions will help to prevent such problems arising.*

ULCER DISEASE

The first signs of ulcers are reddening at the base of the fins, in the anal region and on parts of the body. If left untreated, these reddened areas develop into open wounds. Affected fishes often go off their food.

This bacterial infection is most often seen on newly imported fish that have been badly handled during transportation and consequently have a low resistance to infection. Caught at an early stage, normal antibacterial treatments are effective against ulcers. Should the infection take hold, however, it becomes progressively more difficult to treat and spreads to apparently healthy stock. It is vital to treat the whole aquarium or pond. Feeding a course of flake or pelleted food impregnated with antibiotics will effect a cure, but if the fish have gone off their food it may be necessary to use a bath of an antibacterial remedy such as nifurpirinol at 0.1-0.2mg/litre or a suitable antibiotic solution as recommended for treating finrot. With large fish, antibiotics can be administered by injection, but this is a delicate procedure that your veterinarian should carry out.

Below: *This ulcerated lesion on the body is caused by a bacterial infection. At such an advanced stage, this requires swift treatment.*

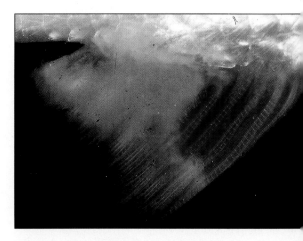

Above: *Signs of fungus. The spores abound in water and will invade damaged tissue if the protective layer of mucus is breached.*

FUNGUS

Fungus usually appears as a fluffy growth on a damaged area of the body or fin. If left untreated, it can spread very quickly and may engulf the entire fish. *Saprolegnia* is one of the species of aquatic fungi responsible.

Good aquarium management will help to prevent fungal infections. The mucus coating on the fish's skin provides a natural protection against attack by fungal spores, but if this mucus layer becomes weakened or damaged by cuts and abrasions or by attack from parasites such as the anchor worm (*Lernaea*), then the spores can invade the tissues and proliferate.

There are several proprietary remedies available for treating fungus and, used as directed, these are very effective if the infection is caught at an early stage. Persistent attacks require more direct treatment. Mercurochrome, an antiseptic available from your veterinarian or pharmacist, may be applied directly to wounds infected with fungus, using a soft paintbrush or a cotton bud. It is not an instant cure and you may need to repeat the treatment. Be sure to take care when using mercurochrome and, ideally, wear a pair of protective gloves. Applying some petroleum jelly to the affected area after painting with mercurochrome will give a waterproof covering to the wound, preventing the antiseptic from being diluted too quickly by the aquarium water.

WHITE SPOT (ICH)

This is probably the first disease that aquarists encounter. The initial signs of infection are small white spots, about 1mm(0.04in) in diameter, scattered on the fins and/or body of the fish. These irritate the fish and cause it to flick against rocks, plants and gravel in a vain attempt to remove the parasites. In fresh water, white spot is caused by the protozoan *Ichthyophthirius multifiliis*, from which it derives its other common name of 'ich'.

To get the most out of the treatment, it is an advantage to understand the life cycle of the parasite involved. The white spots that appear on the fish are individual, single-celled parasites lodged in the uppermost layer of skin and feeding on the host. When these mature, they break out of the skin and become free swimming for a few hours. Eventually they fall to the aquarium or pond floor and form capsules, or cysts, which become attached to the substrate. Within each cyst, the original single cell divides many times until the cyst breaks open to release hundreds of free-swimming stages. These must find a host fish within about 24 hours if they are to survive and complete the cycle. It is only during the free-swimming phases of the life cycle that treatment is effective; once contained in cysts on the fish or on the aquarium substrate, the parasites are immune from the effect of any medications.

There are many proprietary remedies for treating white spot, but take care when using these as some fish show great sensitivity to them. With catfish such as *Loricaria* sp. and *Panaque* sp., or eels of the genus *Mastacemblus*, use these remedies at

The life cycle of white spot

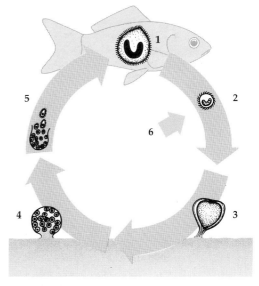

Above: **1** *Individual parasites lodge just underneath the skin.*
2 *Mature parasites punch out of the skin and swim away.*
3 *Each parasite becomes enclosed in a cyst fixed to the substrate floor.*
4 *In the cyst the single cell divides into over 1,000 infective stages.*
5 *The free-swimming stages invade the fins, skin and gills of fish.*
6 *Treatment is only effective against the free-swimming stages.*

Left: *A few white spots are just visible on this Geophagus hondae.*

half the recommended strength. They will take a little longer to work at this strength but will not harm the fish in the process. As an alternative approach, raising the water temperature to at least 32°C(90°F) for a few hours every three to five days will also help to eradicate white spot, if your fish can stand this treatment.

HOLE-IN-THE-HEAD DISEASE

This problem is most often associated with cichlids, although it does occur in some other fishes. Small holes appear, usually in the region of the head, although they can occur near the lateral line or on the bases of the fins. These gradually enlarge and increase, eventually emitting a yellowish mucus that trails through the water.

Hole-in-the-head disease is caused by the protozoan *Hexamita*. This creature may be found in small numbers in the intestines of fish and, under normal circumstances, does no harm. If the fish becomes stressed through incorrect feeding or overcrowding, then the disease may show itself.

Fish have often gone off their food by the time symptoms become apparent, and so the simple method of treating it by feeding it medicated food is pointless. Drugs such as dimetridazole and metronidazole can be used as a continuous bath under veterinary guidance, the former at the rate of 5mg/litre, the latter at 7mg/litre. This treatment may need to be repeated. Approach both these treatments with the utmost care as neither has been tried on a wide variety of fish. There are commercial treatments available that contain dimetridazole and metronidazole, but, once again, use these with care on rare or unusual species.

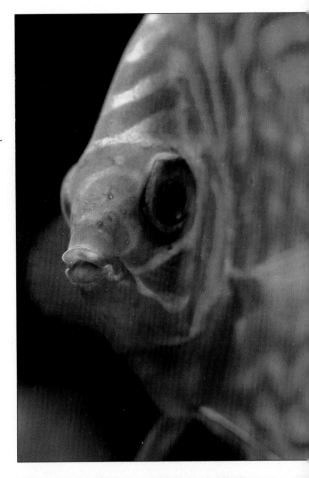

Above: *Signs of the early stages of hole-in-the-head disease on the face of a discus. Without treatment, these holes will gradually enlarge.*

Below: *A single fish louse clinging to the skin. Note the outline of two large suckers on the underside and the small dark eyes on the head.*

FISH LICE

The fish louse (*Argulus*) is commonly seen on coldwater fish but it also attacks tropical species. When inadvertently introduced into the aquarium, it will multiply rapidly.

This crustacean is about 10mm(0.4in) in diameter. It is transparent and easily overlooked, because the colour of the host fish shows through the louse's body. It attaches itself to its host by means of a pair of suckers on its underside and, once in

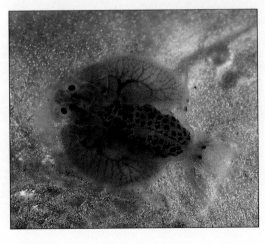

The life cycle of the fish louse

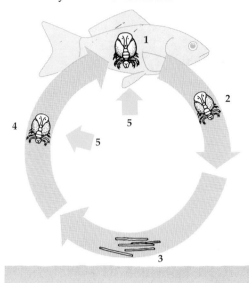

Above: 1 Adults cling to the fish and draw blood through the skin. 2 Mature females drop away to lay their eggs on any hard surface. 3 The eggs are laid in gelatinous capsules a *few centimetres long. 4 In warm conditions, juveniles hatch out in four weeks and mature through several stages. 5 Treating the water should eradicate both adults and juveniles.*

place, is extremely difficult to dislodge. Heavily infested fish will rub against rocks and even leap from the water in an attempt to remove these pests. *Argulus* feeds on blood, and reddish sores may appear where it has been feeding. Treat these with an antiseptic to prevent them becoming points of infection by bacteria and fungus.

An effective way of eradicating fish lice is to use the insecticide metriphonate. Remember to handle this organophosphorous substance with great care. Treat the whole aquarium or pond over a period of 7-10 days, using metriphonate at a strength of 0.25-0.4mg/litre. The substance degrades more quickly in warm alkaline water than it does in cooler (less than 24°C/75°F) acidic conditions. Metriphonate acts on the nervous system. Some fish, such as piranhas, are very sensitive to it and it is essential to remove them from the tank or pond before you start

the treatment. For these sensitive fish use a 30-minute bath of potassium permanganate solution at a strength of 10-20mg/litre of water. This treatment may need repeating.

ANCHOR WORMS

This parasite is rarely a problem on established aquarium fish, but it is often seen on newly imported fish and infestations can occur without warning in pond fish. The anchor worm (*Lernaea*), is an elongate parasite, yellowish in colour, which attaches itself to its host by burying its head deep into the body wall and fixing itself with two anchorlike extensions. It is usually the females that are seen attached to fish; the males die soon after mating.

It is reasonably easy to remove anchor worms with tweezers. Catch the fish and wrap it in a damp linen cloth, leaving the affected part uncovered. Grasp the anchor worm close to the fish's body and gently pull it away. Treat the site of attachment with an antiseptic to prevent secondary infection. If an ulcer has developed at the point of attachment, you can treat this by immersing the fish in a solution of a suitable antibacterial, such as nifurpirinol at 0.1-0.2mg/litre. Treat heavy infestations with metriphonate, as for fish lice.

Below: A female anchor worm, about 2cm(0.8in) long, attached at the *head end. The 'tail' consists of twin eggsacs full to bursting.*

The life cycle of the anchor worm

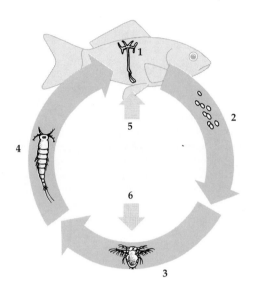

Above: 1 Females only anchor into fish skin.
2 Eggs are released into the water from eggsacs.
3 Free-living juveniles must find fish host.

4 Later parasitic stages mate and the males die.
5 Remove adults with care and treat wounds.
6 Treat the water to eradicate the juveniles.

Below: A fish leech removed from its host. There is a sucker at each end of the elastic body. Leeches can transmit microbial infections.

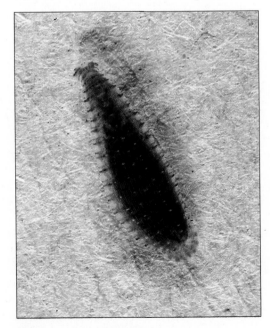

LEECHES

There are many species of leech, some of which are predatory and others parasitic; it is the parasitic species that attack fish. They feed by sucking blood, and move with a looping motion, using the two suckers, one at either end of the distensible body. Any attack by a parasite will weaken its host, and the leech is no exception, heavy infestations invariably leading to the death of the affected fish.

It is possible to cope with minor attacks of one or two leeches on an individual fish by removing them with tweezers and painting the attachment wounds with a suitable antiseptic. Leeches may also be removed by giving the fish a salt bath of 20-30gm/litre for 15-30 minutes, and then treating the wounds with antiseptic. Alternatively, treat the whole aquarium or pond with metriphonate as for fish lice.

The life cycle of the fish leech

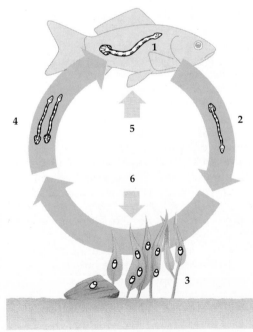

Above: 1 Adult leeches draw blood from fish.
2 They leave the fish to digest meal or lay eggs.
3 Eggs in oval cocoons on plants and rocks.
4 Once hatched, the

leeches must seek out a suitable fish host.
5 Treat infested fishes with a salt bath or a suitable remedy.
6 Drain and discard plants to control eggs.

INTESTINAL WORMS

These are not normally visible externally, but heavy infestations do become apparent when the worms protrude from the vent of the fish. The worm that usually causes the most problems in the confines of an aquarium or pond is the roundworm *Camallanus*. It is usually introduced into the aquarium in newly imported fish and, once there, is capable of reproducing without the intermediate hosts usually involved in its life cycle. It may also be introduced with infected live foods, such as the copepod crustaceans that form its intermediate host. The infection may be spread by other fishes eating the faeces of an infected fish that contain juvenile *Camallanus*, or, on occasion through cannibalism.

Treatment may be difficult and it is advisable to seek the advice of your veterinarian. Piperazine citrate has been used with some success on small livebearers by mixing it with flaked food at a rate of 25mg/10gm food and feeding it over a period of 5-10 days. Levamisole is used to treat infestations of internal worms in a wide variety of animals. For affected fish it can be used at the rate of 200mg/kg of body weight, and can be injected or absorbed from the water. Whatever course of treatment you choose, please remember that little is known about the effects of these substances on many tropical species and they should only be administered with caution under strict veterinary control.

The possible infection cycles of the intestinal worm *Camallanus*

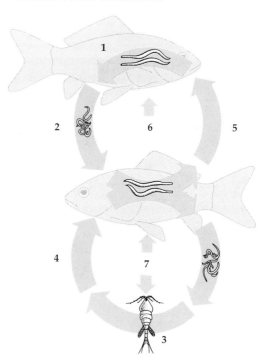

Above: **1** *Adult worms live in the intestine.*
2 *Juveniles in faeces are ingested by other fish.*
3 *Juveniles may also be eaten by copepods.*
4 *Infected copepods become the food of fish.*

5 *A fish may eat other fish already infected.*
6 *Treat affected fish with suitable drugs.*
7 *Remove dead fish to prevent cannibalism and avoid feeding fish with any suspect live foods.*

Below: A close view of the mouthparts of a Camallanus *worm, showing the tiny jaws and muscular throat.*

Right: The upturned body of a fish with a cluster of red-brown Camallanus *worms showing at the vent.*

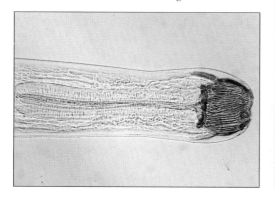

A SELECTION OF FISHES

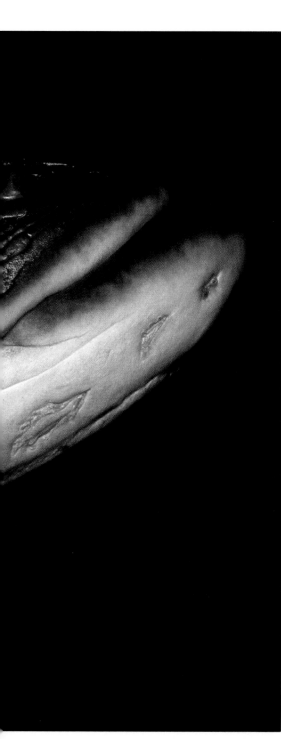

The fishes included in this section fall into three main categories: they may be species that grow to a large size and therefore require a large tank; there are the active shoaling fish that do not necessarily grow very long, but require a large tank to provide plenty of swimming space; and finally, there are the naturally territorial species that require their own 'patch'.

To make the most of this book, make sure that you read this section in conjunction with the early chapters. Pay special attention to the filtration and water requirements of the fish, for example, as this is an area in which many problems can arise. Equally important are your own views on what to feed your fish. Many fish will take frozen or pelleted foods, whereas others will be vegetarians, happy to consume peas and lettuce. However, a few fishes require live foods. Before assuming responsibility for representatives of this group, you should realize that you will have to feed them live fish or watch them starve. This may be necessary for only a few weeks until the fish has been persuaded to accept dead foods, but it is a matter for your conscience. If you cannot do it, then perhaps it would be wise to think again about the choice of fish for your aquarium.

Given good conditions, large fishes are long-lived, many surviving for at least 10 years in captivity and some for considerably longer. This calls for a whole-hearted commitment on your part, so it is vital to choose the most appropriate fish and aquarium system from the beginning.

This selection of fishes includes something for everyone – peaceful vegetarian species, voracious predators, those that will breed in the right conditions, and those that will become a family pet. In each case, full details of their basic requirements are included. The final choice is up to you.

Left: *The magnificent head of* Arapaima gigas, *one of the largest freshwater fishes, reaching 4m(13.1ft) in the Amazon River.*

LUNGFISHES

The lungfishes can be traced back through the fossil record to the Lower Devonian period (about 400 million years ago). Today, they are represented by three genera: *Lepidosiren* has one species, *L. paradoxa*, from the fresh waters of Brazil and Paraguay; *Neoceratodus*, also with one, *N. forsteri*, in the fresh waters of southern Queensland; and *Protopterus*, which has four species widespread in the fresh waters of Africa. In all these elongate fishes, the dorsal, caudal and anal fins are united. It is interesting to note that the distribution of this ancient group is very similar to that of the bony tongues, and probably stems from the break up of the supercontinent Gondwanaland and the movement of the continents to the positions they hold today.

LEPIDOSIREN PARADOXA
South American lungfish

Size: 1.25m(4.1ft).
Distribution: Central South America.

Juvenile specimens have yellow blotches that fade as they mature; adults are dark grey with small scales. The unrayed pectoral and ventral fins are filamentous and short. These fish are capable of breathing air using the paired airbladder and adults are reported to aestivate (become dormant) under adverse (i.e. dry) conditions.

In captivity, *Lepidosiren* is a very placid fish, especially compared to its African cousin, and quite tolerant of other fishes. Feeding is straightforward, as the South American lungfish will accept commercially available frozen foods, as well as pelleted foods. Aquatic snails and earthworms are a great delicacy. A water temperature of 20-24°C(68-75°F) is ideal.

Below: The external filamentous breathing organs of Lepidosiren paradoxa *regress at a very early age. Even this specimen, measuring only 5cm(2in) long, lacks the breathing organ.*

Lepidosiren creates a burrow at the bottom of swamps for spawning. At this time, the males develop many branched filaments on their ventral fins and some authorities believe that these are accessory breathing organs. However, another theory maintains that they are placed among the eggs so that oxygen from the bloodstream diffuses out of them to the developing eggs. In common with *Protopterus*, the larvae have four pairs of external gills and undergo the same metamorphosis to reach their adult form.

NEOCERATODUS FORSTERI
Australian lungfish

Size: 1.75m(5.7ft).
Distribution: Queensland, Australia.

The Australian lungfish is included here in order to present a more complete picture of this family of fishes, but *N. forsteri* is not available commercially and is so rare in Australia that it is a protected species. The Australian lungfish differs in appearance from its African and South American cousins in that large scales cover a more compressed body and the paired fins are more paddlelike. Internally, the airbladder

Above: Neoceratodus forsteri *is now a protected species in its native Australia and not* *available to the fish-keeping hobby. It may be possible to see examples in a public aquarium.*

is unpaired. Adults do not aestivate.

Neoceratodus spawns among aquatic plants, and the male carries out the brood care. On hatching, the young have no external gills. In 1989 an Australian newspaper, the Sydney Morning Herald, carried a report of the first successful attempt to breed these fish in a garden pond. 'Occasionally the younger ones will clamber up onto a rock in the pond, using their front fins as legs, to breathe in the fresh air. They may look around at the other animals, or out to the sea nearby, but as soon as anyone comes near they disappear again into the depths of the pond.' Subsequent reports described adult fish in the wild 'walking' in a similar manner to a seal, raising the body on the pectoral fins and pushing with the ventral fins. Smaller specimens were seen jumping around in the shallows, much like frogs. The fish were most active at dawn and dusk, presumably because there were too many predators about for them to leave the safety of the water during the day.

PROTOPTERUS ANNECTENS
African lungfish

Size: Up to 85cm(33.5in).
Distribution: Widespread throughout West Africa.

The dark brown body of this very robust fish is covered with very small scales and the long, filamentous pectoral and anal fins are without rays.

P. annectens is the most aggressive of the lungfishes in captivity. Take particular care when cleaning and maintaining the aquarium, as it will not hesitate to use its powerful jaws to bite anything that moves, even the hand that feeds it! An external power filter is adequate and additional aeration unnecessary. The African lungfish is not too fussy about water conditions, but avoid extremes of pH and hardness. The temperature in the aquarium can vary in the range 18-30°C(64-86°F).

The African lungfish will eat just about anything, including its tankmates, if the opportunity arises. Offer it a wide variety of foods, such as insect larvae, larger crustaceans – either live river shrimp (*Palaemonetes varians*) or dead shrimps and prawns (complete with shells) – pieces of fish and meat, earthworms and maggots.

When the watercourses dry up in its natural habitat during the hottest months of the year, the lungfish is able to breathe air, using the paired airbladder as a lung. If conditions deteriorate further, adults aestivate during the dry season, remaining in this state for up to two years until the rains return. The fish burrow into the mud and bend their bodies into a U-shape so that the mouth and tail are both at the top of the burrow. Then they secrete a mucous sheath around themselves, leaving an air passage to the surface. The sheath hardens to prevent the fish from becoming desiccated and when the waters return the mucus becomes soft, allowing a somewhat emaciated lungfish to emerge.

The African lungfish breeds at the beginning of the rainy season, in mudholes clear of aquatic vegetation. Its eggs are large and surrounded by a gelatinous membrane, similar to that seen on frogspawn. The male guards the spawn and the newly hatched young, which are able to stick to the substrate or plants by means of adhesive organs. The larvae have four pairs of feathery external gills and resemble young newts until they assume their adult form at about two to three months old.

Above: *Belligerent, bellicose, quarrelsome – these are just some of the kinder adjectives that describe the African lungfish,* P. annectens.

Left: *In the wild, the waters inhabited by* Protopterus *dry out seasonally and the fish must undergo a period of aestivation to survive.*

Below: *Before the mud becomes parched,* Protopterus *burrows vertically down, turns back on itself, covers the entrance with mud, but leaves small holes for respiration. It excretes a mucus that encapsulates the fish and prevents desiccation. This species can live semi-dormant for months or years.*

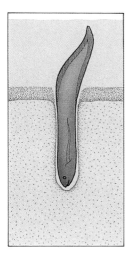
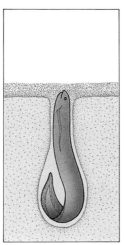
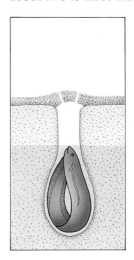
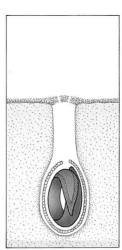

STURGEONS

The sturgeons are a primitive group of fishes characterized by a cartilaginous skeleton, heterocercal tail (i.e. with one lobe – the upper – larger than the other) and

The heterocercal tail

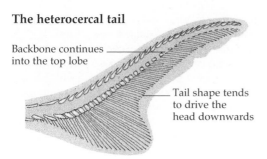

Backbone continues into the top lobe

Tail shape tends to drive the head downwards

rows of heavy plates along the flanks and dorsal surface. Fossils of this ancient group have been found in Montana, USA, and have been dated as being from the Upper Cretaceous period (approximately 135-65 million years ago). A few species are found in North America but a greater number occur in Europe and the USSR, with some in China. Most are freshwater, but those that do live in the sea return to fresh waters to spawn. The beluga (*Huso huso*) is a sturgeon well known for being the largest freshwater fish (old records up to 8m/26ft, nowadays to 4.2m/13.8ft) and also because of the high-quality caviar of its eggs.

ACIPENSER RUTHENUS
Sterlet

Size: Up to 90m(36in).
Distribution: Europe and Siberia, tributaries of the Black Sea, Caspian Sea and Sea of Azov. It is also found in some tributaries of the Baltic Sea.

These fish are most unusual to look at, and rightly attract a great deal of interest. The body is silvery grey above, with five rows of heavy bony plates. The mouth is located on the underside of the long pointed head, behind four barbels that hang down from the snout. These tactile barbels are covered with 'taste' sensors and are held out so that they just touch the substrate as the fish skims along searching for food. As soon as it senses a tasty morsel, it stirs up the sediment and consumes its bottom-dwelling prey. Because of the sensitivity of the barbels and the sterlet's method of feeding, it is vital to provide a substrate of rounded particles of sand in the aquarium. Avoid sharp rocks and stones to prevent the fish damaging the barbels.

Small specimens are offered for sale in aquarium shops and these will acclimatize readily to aquarium conditions. Provide plenty of space and maintain the clear, cold

water at 12-15°C(54-59°F), although this may be allowed to rise to 22-24°C(72-75°F) during the summer. Should the water become warmer, the fish may suffer from lack of

Above: Acipenser *uses its barbels, covered in taste sensors, to judge the proximity of food.*

Below: Acipenser ruthenus *prefers cool, clear well-oxygenated water in the aquarium.*

oxygen and you will need to place additional water circulation pumps in the aquarium. When temperatures do rise, it is a good idea to place blocks of ice (made in old ice-cream containers) in the tank and the fish will cavort contentedly in the cool water as the ice melts. A pH value of 7.5 and a general hardness of 10-15°dH are suitable. Large external power filters are necessary, not only to create a strong current of water in the aquarium, but also to deal with the large amount of dust and debris that sterlets inevitably churn up when feeding. Install a biological, undertank filter to maintain water quality. (An undergravel filter would be disrupted by the fish's feeding method.)

Sterlets are harmless and peaceful with fishes of their own size, but they are not averse to eating small fishes if these happen to be in the aquarium. Preferred foods are insect larvae, *Tubifex* worms and snails, but they will take flaked and pelleted foods. Sometimes, sterlets like to bury themselves in the substrate, so allow open areas of sand, free from plants and rocks, to accommodate them.

Sterlets are unlikely to breed in the aquarium. In the wild, they spawn over gravel beds during May and June, producing 11,000-135,000 eggs that hatch within four to five days.

PADDLEFISHES

The paddlefishes – family Polyodontidae – are represented by two genera, each with a single species: *Polyodon spathula* from the Mississippi river system in North America and *Psephurus gladius* from the Changjiang (Yangtze River) in China. Both species are only found in fresh waters and are large – *Polyodon spathula* reaching 2.2m(7ft 3in) and *Psephurus gladius* 7m(23ft). Interestingly, the gill rakers in *P. spathula* are long and numerous, whereas in *P. gladius*, although still relatively large and numerous when compared to other fishes, they are fewer and smaller than in *P. spathula*. Both species are highly prized as food fishes. Here, we look at *Polyodon*, the North American river species, as the Chinese species is unlikely to be imported for the aquarium market.

POLYODON SPATHULA
Paddlefish

Size: Up to 2.2m(7.3ft).
Distribution: Mississippi River system, Mobile Bay drainage, Alabama west to eastern Texas.

The paddlefish is probably the most easily recognized of all North American fishes, with the snout elongated to form the thin, flat paddle reflected in its common name. It is the most prominent feature and forms approximately a quarter of the fish's entire length. The body is slightly compressed and

Below: *The very large gape of* Polyodon spathula *belies the fact that this is a plankton feeder, straining its food through gill rakers in front of gill filaments.*

Above: P. spathula *requires plenty of open swimming space in the aquarium and an abundance of plankton, such as* Daphnia, *to survive in captivity.*

covered in a smooth, grey skin very similar to the skin found on freshwater catfishes. Whereas catfishes lack scales, however, paddlefish do have some diamond-shaped scales, but only on the caudal peduncle; the rest of the body is naked. The coloration is more intense on the back, becoming lighter on the flanks, and the belly region is white. The eyes are small, typical of a fish living in the silt-laden waters of the Mississippi River, and are located just above the snout. They are of little use to the paddlefish and, to compensate for this diminution in sight, the snout has developed into a highly sensitive organ. There is a large tapering opercular flap extending to the ventral fins. The caudal fin is deeply forked, which aids the fish when cruising in midwater to feed.

The mouth of *Polyodon spathula* is cavernous and armed with minute teeth. It feeds by swimming through clouds of plankton, sweeping its head from side to side. Vast amounts of plankton are strained through the many close-set gill rakers, which can be clearly seen when the mouth is held wide open as it feeds. It uses the highly sensitive, paddle-shaped snout to locate the plankton and orientate itself in the murky waters in which it lives. The snout is reported to be used to sweep through mud in order to stir up any minute organisms that it can consume. The paddle may also act as a stabilizer when the fish is swimming with its mouth open during feeding. In the aquarium, it is vital to provide vast amounts of *Daphnia* or other

Above: *A juvenile paddlefish. Sudden movements can alarm the fish. Select decor with care to avoid damage to the delicate snout.*

Left: *The extremely sensitive spade-shaped snout is used to locate food, and may also act as a stabilizer when feeding.*

minute organisms to keep this fish well fed and healthy.

Paddlefish were once widespread in the USA, but pollution and destruction of habitat have reduced their range. Their export was restricted but, with the advent of commercial breeding programmes (paddlefish make excellent eating), they are now available for export. Normally offered for sale at around 10cm(4in), they command a high price. They also command great dedication from the aquarist in maintaining a regular and plentiful supply of food. (See page 40 for further advice on feeding.)

The delicate snout is easily damaged, both in transit and in the aquarium, so always take great care not to frighten these fishes. They like dimly lit conditions with gentle water movement. In the wild, they are found in quiet backwaters; turbulent waters would quickly sweep away the clouds of plankton on which they feed.

Since *P. spathula* is very active, allow plenty of swimming space in the aquarium and make sure that there are no sharp objects on which the fish could damage themselves. Use sand as the substrate, and, ideally, filter the water through an undertank, biological system. Provide a temperature range of 10-18°C(50-64°F).

Paddlefish are known to make spawning runs upriver, and at this time they make excellent sport for fishermen. It is unlikely that they will spawn in the home aquarium.

GARPIKES

These ancient pikelike fishes have been in existence since the Mesozoic era (about 245-64 million years ago), but today only seven species in two genera are found in North and Central America and Cuba. The slim cylindrical body is covered with small diamond-shaped, ganoid scales that effectively encase the body in a form of armour. (Ganoid scales are heavy and inflexible 'primitive' forerunners of the elasmoid scales of 'modern' bony fish.) Since they do not overlap, these scales restrict the fish's flexibility. A joint behind the skull enables the garpike to make nodding head movements. The fins are small, the caudal fin being rounded.

During the summer, when saturated oxygen levels decrease due to the increased water temperature, the swimbladder assumes a secondary function as an accessory respiratory organ. At these times, the jaws are pushed far out of the water.

The sharp teeth in their elongated jaws are an indication of these fishes' predatory nature. In the wild, garpikes feed almost exclusively on small fishes. To avoid entanglement when handling garpikes, use a heavy linen net and take care not to become caught on the fearsome teeth or to cut your hands on the sharp scales.

In the spawning season, from March to May, adhesive eggs attach themselves to plants or the substrate. On hatching, the larvae hang vertically, using a sucker on the upper jaw, and remain suspended until the yolk sac is absorbed. The fry develop rapidly. There are no reports of garpikes spawning in a home aquarium, but gars have been bred in Florida and Georgia. They have also been hybridized – *L. oculatus* being crossed with *L. platyrhincus*.

Garpikes range in size from the 90cm(36in) spotted gar (*Lepisosteus oculatus*) to the 3m(10ft) alligator gar (*Atractosteus spatula*). Here, we look at two species that can be kept in an aquarium.

Below left: *Diamond-shaped, enamel-like ganoid scales lie side by side and allow the fish's body little flexibility.*

Below: *Front edges of elasmoid scales are embedded in skin; the rear edges overlap next scale, so allow flexing.*

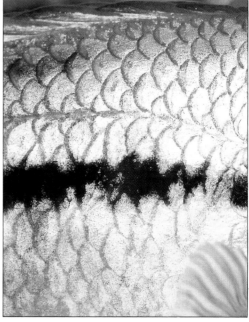

LEPISOSTEUS OCULATUS
Spotted gar

Size: Up to 90cm(36in).
Distribution: Lake Erie and southern Lake Michigan drainages; Mississippi River drainage from Illinois to eastern Oklahoma and eastern Tennessee; streams draining into the Gulf of Mexico from central Texas to western Florida.

Adult spotted gars have a brown to olive dorsal surface, with somewhat lighter flanks and a whitish belly. The head and body are peppered with darker spots that continue into the fins. Indeed, the specific name oculatus means 'provided with eyes', referring to these spots. Juveniles have a dark mid-dorsal and mid-lateral stripe. One of the ways of identifying this species is by the short snout, which is less than twice as long as the rest of the head. The upper jaw is armed with a single row of teeth.

 L. oculatus lurks among vegetation in deeper, clear pools, swamps, streams and lakes throughout its range. At the southern extent of its range, along the Gulf of Mexico, it may be found in brackish water regions. Maintain and feed this species in the same way as Lepisosteus osseus.

LEPISOSTEUS OSSEUS
Longnose gar

Size: Up to 1.8m(5.9ft).
Distribution: The most widespread of the gars, being found in the St. Lawrence drainage system; along the Atlantic coast south of New Jersey to Orlando, Florida; from the southern Great Lakes and Mississippi River system, south to the Rio Grande drainage system in Texas.

When adult, the longnose gar is dark green-brown dorsally, with lighter flanks covered with dark spots near the tail and a creamy white belly. The dorsal, caudal and anal fins are light brown with dark spots. Juveniles are similar, but have a dark stripe along the dorsal surface and one along the flanks. The most distinctive characteristic of *Lepisosteus osseus* is the long snout, which is more than twice as long as the rest of the head. It is

Below: *Two or three* Atractosteus oculatus *make a good focal point in a show tank. Given sufficient plant cover for security, they will always be on show.*

Right: Lepisosteus osseus, *a much larger garpike, must be treated with respect. Mature specimens can easily dislodge cover glasses and damage themselves.*

sometimes damaged and liable to fungal and bacterial infections. The teeth occur in a single row on the upper jaw.

Although considered a game fish, it is rarely eaten because the roe is poisonous. In summer, the longnose gar can be seen lying motionless 'innocently' at the surface in quiet backwaters, but it can cause damage to fish stocks and its teeth become entangled in the fine mesh of nets. This also makes it difficult to catch.

Juveniles make attractive aquarium fish, but have a tendency to be skittish and can jump at the slightest provocation. A well-established planted aquarium is ideal for *Lepisosteus osseus*. It tolerates a wide range of water temperatures, but does require well-filtered water and only moderate turbulence. The fish lurk among the plants, where their coloration renders them almost invisible. Floating vegetation or lily pads give them a greater feeling of security and help to suppress their urge to leap. However, the resultant lack of light is a disadvantage to the other water plants and it is important to strike a careful balance.

BOWFINS

Bowfins are an ancient group of fishes in the order Amiiformes. They flourished during the Jurassic and Cretaceous periods and fossils are known from Europe, Asia and North America. They have a primitive skeleton composed of bone and cartilage, but certain features are more characteristic of modern bony fishes. These include vertebrae that are concave at each end, thin bony plates on the head, cycloid (i.e. thin and rounded) scales on the body and a rounded tail with just a hint of the ancient heterocercal shape. The family Amiidae is represented by one species, the predatory *Amia calva*.

AMIA CALVA

Size: Up to 90cm(36in).
Distribution: North America, in Lake Champlain, St. Lawrence River west through the Great Lakes; Mississippi River system; Minnesota to Texas; Long Island; Coastal Plain, southern Pennsylvania to Florida, west to Texas.

Its natural coloration makes *Amia* well suited to a predatory lifestyle among water plants. The long-based fins are all dark olive green, but the flanks are lighter green with a darker olive lacework pattern, and the belly is cream to very pale green. The lateral line is complete. In males, the caudal fin has a conspicuous spot in its upper portion, ringed with bright yellow or orange. There are two tubular nostrils and, as befits a piscivore, numerous teeth in the jaws.

In the wild, the bowfin lives in clear, slow-moving waters, swamps and oxbow lakes with abundant vegetation, but this hardy coldwater species is often considered a nuisance, preying on the small fishes intended for introduced game fishes. In the aquarium, the bowfin needs space to hunt and an efficient filtration system that will keep the water clear and well oxygenated. Although it can tolerate low oxygen levels, using its swimbladder as an accessory breathing organ, problems can occur in the aquarium when the temperature rises during a hot summer and oxygen levels decrease. For this reason, the optimum temperature for aquarium specimens is 12-22°C(54-72°F) and a power filter with a spraybar return will help to maintain adequate oxygen levels. (Below 12°C, *Amia* becomes less active, grows at a slower rate and requires less food.) There is no reason why you should not keep a bowfin in a reasonably sized garden pond, provided the pool is deep enough not to freeze solid in the winter.

Feeding is not usually a problem, since bowfins come to accept most meaty foods, such as prawn, fish and small pieces of meat. Young fishes adapt more easily to

aquarium conditions, although it may be necessary to offer them live food in the form of small fishes during the acclimatization period and wean them onto other foods at a later stage. Larger specimens, accustomed to live prey, may prove more difficult to introduce, but will eventually settle down given a good supply of food fish.

Bowfins spawn in shallow waters during early spring. The male clears the vegetation, creating a shallow depression in the substrate. He also guards the eggs until they hatch and protects the young for several weeks. Captive breeding is most likely to be achieved in a garden pool; aquarium breeding has not been recorded.

Right: Bowfins are inquisitive fishes and will become quite tame. With a little patience, they can be encouraged to feed from their keeper's hand, taking a variety of meaty foods offered to them.

Below: Although not often offered for sale, Amia calva makes a welcome addition to the larger coldwater tank. Choose tankmates with care – the bowfin has a predatory nature.

KNIFEFISHES

Within the knifefishes – Family Notopteridae – the two genera most often encountered by aquarists are, *Notopterus* from tropical Africa and Southeast Asia and *Xenomystus* from tropical Africa. Both are elongate, compressed fishes with a long anal fin united with the small caudal fin to form the main propulsion unit. Using wavelike motions of this fin, the fishes are able to move easily forwards or backwards to catch their prey or avoid predation. The body is covered with small scales. The mouth is large and has many small teeth, and there are two tubular nostrils on the snout. The two genera can be distinguished by the presence or absence of a dorsal fin: *Notopterus* has it, *Xenomystus* does not. Here we consider *Notopterus chitala*.

NOTOPTERUS CHITALA
Clown knifefish

Size: Up to 80cm(32in); in the past they have been recorded at over 100cm(39in).
Distribution: India, Burma, Thailand, Malaya, Java, Sumatra and Borneo.

Notopterus chitala is a very attractive fish for the home aquarium. Those specimens coming from Thailand are the most beautifully marked, having a line of black spots, usually with a well-defined white ring around each, along the flanks. The

Above: *Several species of* Notopterus *are known, but all have a similar body shape and share the same general requirements. This* Notopterus vittatus *comes from Thailand.*

Left: *A quiet river in Southeast Asia, the typical habitat of* Notopterus *knifefishes.*

Right: *Larger examples of* Notopterus chitala *are sometimes offered for sale by an inexperienced aquarist who has found that these fishes have flourished on a diet of his community fishes!*

number of spots can vary, both from individual to individual (usually there are 5 to 10 on each side) and from side to side of the same fish (by one or two spots). Those specimens from the islands forming the Indo-Australian Archipelago (Sumatra, Java, Borneo, etc.) only rarely show this spotting on the body.

The clown knifefish lives in rivers, canals and swamps, where it often swims near the surface, occasionally breaking the surface and rolling on its side to expose a large silvery flank. It is a carnivore, feeding on insects, shrimps and small, surface-swimming fishes.

In the aquarium, juveniles readily accept pieces of shrimp, fish and meat. It is an avid feeder and produces large amounts of high-protein waste, so an efficient biological filtration system is essential. Since its natural habitats are swamps and slow-moving bodies of water, *N. chitala* will cope with most water conditions and will tolerate higher temperatures than those considered the norm for tropical aquarium fishes. During breeding, for example, an average water temperature of 33°C(91°F) has been recorded (see right).

The clown knife can be quarrelsome, even among its own kind, and needs plenty of space in the aquarium. If two or three small specimens are grown on together there is less likelihood of fighting than if a semi-mature individual is introduced to an already established specimen or group.

Throughout their range, these fishes are highly regarded as a food fish. In Thailand in 1932, the Siamese Bureau of Fisheries encouraged them to spawn by providing wooden posts driven into the substrate of the backwaters and swamps on which the females could lay their eggs. Not all the posts were utilised by the fishes but on those that were, several thousand eggs were deposited at any one spawning. Spawning takes place during May, June and July. After laying, the female plays no further part in caring for the brood. The male guards the eggs, fanning them with his tail to prevent sediment from the silt-laden waters settling on them and thus rendering them open to fungal attack. At this time, the male is very protective and will attack and drive away anything, be it fish or human, that intrudes on his territory. At an average water temperature of 33°C(91°F) the eggs hatch within 5 to 6 days.

Being so popular as a food fish, *Notopterus chitala* is often shipped hundreds of miles to market in water-filled barges. The flesh is reputed to have a fine flavour but it contains many small bones.

BONY TONGUES

Fossil records of this ancient and widespread family of fishes date back to the Eocene epoch (approximately 55-35 million years ago) in North America and Sumatra and to the Tertiary period (approximately 65-10 million years ago) in Australia and India. Today, they are represented by *Osteoglossum bicirrhosum*, *O. ferreirai* and *Arapaima gigas* in South America; by *Heterotis niloticus* in Africa, and in the Indo-Australian region by three species of *Scleropages*: *S. formosus*, *S. leichardtii* and *S. jardini*. All the members of this family are found in large bodies of fresh water.

In this family of fishes, the head is bony and the elongate body is covered by large, heavy scales, with a mosaic pattern of canals. The dorsal and anal fins have soft rays and are long based, while the pectoral and ventral fins are small. The fourth gill arch is modified into a helical (screw-shaped) organ, which was once thought to be an extra breathing organ. In 1955, however, research showed that *Heterotis* sp. uses it for filter feeding, trapping fine particles in mucus before swallowing. The name 'bony tongues' is derived from a toothed bone on the floor of the mouth, the 'tongue', equipped with teeth that bite against teeth on the roof of the mouth. The swimbladder is connected to the pharynx by a duct and is used for respiration.

Bony tongues are extremely active, often swimming with sinuous body movements. Their active lifestyle requires well-oxygenated waters, so combine a biological trickle filter with a power filter to create the water flow that these fishes enjoy. As well

as being active, bony tongues are often very nervous, reacting to sudden external movements by dashing around the aquarium and jumping, so be sure to provide a secure cover. Not surprisingly, they are liable to injure themselves and the loss of scales or cuts and bruising to the head and body are not uncommon. In a well-maintained aquarium, a healthy fish will soon recover but, occasionally, it may be necessary to treat wounds for fungal infections (see page 44).

When bony tongues are first introduced into the aquarium, they will often eat only live foods. However, it is possible to wean them onto other foods once they have settled in, and small pieces of fish or meat, prawns and even vegetable matter in the form of lettuce and peas are accepted with relish. Feed these predators no more than three times a week. The species featured here, although not frequently offered for sale, are truly majestic and impressive fishes for the large aquarium.

ARAPAIMA GIGAS
Arapaima

Size: Up to 4m(13.1ft).
Distribution: The Amazon River system.

This is one of the largest freshwater fishes in the world and a truly magnificent creature. The compressed elongate body is covered with large scales and the many sensory canals on the bony head give it a sculptured look. Coloration is variable; the head is iridescent green, with the body a darker blue-green on the dorsal surface (including the dorsal fin) and shading through a greenish coloration on the flanks to a paler belly. The caudal fin is dark. Red-edged scales are particularly prominent at the back of the body. Throughout its range, the arapaima is a high-quality food fish.

A. gigas grows rapidly in captivity and soon becomes a very powerful swimmer and jumper, spending much of its time cruising around the aquarium with sinuous body movements. Feeding is much the same as for *Osteoglossum*; allow a period of fasting each week. The arapaima requires well-filtered, highly oxygenated water and, preferably, slightly soft and acidic conditions. A temperature in the region of 24°C(75°F) is ideal. This fish is probably best suited to a large public aquarium.

The arapaima spawns from January to March, selecting an area with a sandy substrate where it can hollow out a nest about 50cm(20in) in diameter and 15cm(6in) deep. The female deposits an average of 4,000 dark blue-green eggs, approximately 3mm(0.1in) in diameter; these are brooded in the mouth. There is some difference of opinion as to whether it is the male or the female that develops white tubercules on the head at this time. The purpose of these tubercules is unknown, but as the young frequently swarm around the heads of their parents it may be that they provide nourishment or holdfasts for the fry. *Arapaima gigas*, has been bred in large indoor vats in Germany and in man-made lakes in Peru.

Left: *The arapaima is most imposing, but only consider it for the home* *aquarium if you can supply an equally grand life support system.*

OSTEOGLOSSUM BICIRRHOSUM

Size: Up to 1m(39in).
Distribution: Guyana, and the Orinoco and Amazon Basin.

The grey-green *Osteoglossum bicirrhosum* has an iridescent sheen, and each scale is marked with a reddish spot. The fins are slightly lighter in colour, sometimes with faint markings, and in adult specimens the throat may be golden. The strongly compressed body has a keeled belly and the steeply angled mouth opens like a drawbridge. The two forked barbels on the lower jaw are used to detect the struggling movements of insects at the water surface.

In captivity, provide a large, sparsely planted aquarium, with soft, moderately acid water and a temperature of about 25°C(77°F). Young fishes are lively, easy to acclimatize to aquarium conditions and grow rapidly when fed on small fishes and insect larvae. They are particularly fond of

Above: Osteoglossum bicirrhosum *patrols the upper levels of the tank for tasty morsels on the surface of the water.*

Below: A really hungry O. bicirrhosum *turns on its side and flips food items off the substrate before eating them.*

dragonfly nymphs, but make sure these are eaten straight away or they may hide in the tank and attack the fish, causing irritating small wounds open to fungal infection.

In the wild, large numbers of *Osteoglossum bicirrhosum* inhabit weedy backwaters and shallow lakes, swimming at the water surface. They are prodigious jumpers, leaping as much as 2m(6.6ft) out of the water to feed on terrestrial insects. In the aquarium at Blijdorp Zoo, Rotterdam, the public can gaze into a large pool containing *Osteoglossum*, which occasionally jump out of the water, especially when a sparrow dares to perch on an overhanging branch!

O. bicirrhosum is a mouthbrooder and, interestingly, it is the male that incubates the eggs and young for about 60 days. When released, the young measure 6-8cm(2.4-3.2in). Imports sometimes include smaller specimens that have been taken prematurely from their parent's mouth and have not absorbed the yolk sac. At this stage, they are very delicate, but as long as the yolk sac is not damaged they can be kept alive and carefully fed on small live foods. Aquarium breeding is unlikely with these large osteoglossids.

OSTEOGLOSSUM FERREIRAI
Black aruana

Size: Up to 100cm(39in).
Distribution: Rio Negro, South America.

The striking gold and black coloration of this fish is the only feature that distinguishes it from the very similar *O. bicirrhosum*. The body is dark brown to black, with a gold stripe that runs from just behind the gills, along the flanks and into the upper rays of the caudal fin. The remainder of the caudal fin is dark brown to black, as are all the other fins. The head is lighter, with a dark band running from the snout, through the eye to the operculum. The barbels are golden. Care in captivity and breeding strategy are the same as for *O. bicirrhosum* (see page 70).

Below: *The classic lines of the black aruana are enhanced by its fine* *coloration. It makes a delightful addition to the home aquarium.*

HETEROTIS NILOTICUS

Size: Up to 90cm(36in).
Distribution: Upper Nile; rivers of Chad, Niger, Senegal and Gambia.

Heterotis niloticus is the only African representative of the family Osteoglossidae, and is sometimes available to the aquarist. The head and body are a uniform greenish brown and covered in large scales.

This is a filter feeder, consuming mostly plankton and algae, but it will also take larger items. It may be difficult to feed when first introduced into the aquarium but, with patience, it can be coaxed into eating dead foods and taking frozen bloodworms, tablets and other processed foods. Young specimens are easier to acclimatize to the confines of a tank than larger fish that have become set in their dietary habits. Provided the water is well oxygenated and clean, the fish will tolerate a wide range of pH and water hardness levels. Good filtration is essential and a temperature range of 24-30°C(75-86°F) ideal.

Below: *This juvenile specimen of* Heterotis niloticus *is typical of those offered for sale. At 10-12cm(4-4.7in) they are easier to transport and acclimatize to aquarium conditions.*

Towards the end of July, *H. niloticus* constructs a nest in swampy areas close to the main river. This measures about 1.2m(almost 4ft) in diameter and has thick walls of mud and vegetation. The eggs – about 2.5mm(0.1in) in diameter – are deposited in the nest and guarded by the parents until they hatch, about two days later. The larvae have external gills. As with the other large osteoglossids the only chance of successful captive breeding is in ponds in their native countries.

SCLEROPAGES FORMOSUS

Size: Up to 90cm(36in).
Distribution: S. Thailand, S. Vietnam, Malay Peninsula, Sumatra and Indonesia.

This is the most commonly seen species of the genus *Scleropages*. Its colour can vary considerably, from olive brown along the back with greenish to silvery sides and pale green finnage to a deep bronze and red, the latter being the most highly prized. The fin rays are often darker brown. The body of this very beautiful fish is compressed, and the sharply inclined mouth has a wide gape with two small barbels on the chin.
S. formosus is highly valued as a food fish,

72

Above: *If frightened, or feeding on terrestrial insects,* S. formosus *will bend its body into an S-shape before leaping from the water.*

Below: *The mouth of* Scleropages *is very similar in shape to that of* Osteoglossum bicirrhosum *and the gape is equally large.*

its flesh having a good flavour. Large specimens can weigh up to 7.2kg(15.9lb).

In captivity, *Scleropages formosus* requires much the same conditions as *Osteoglossum bicirrhosum*. It is a carnivore and young specimens are very active, so provide a good cover for the aquarium.

In nature, *S. formosus* is found in slow-moving, weedy streams, canals and swamps, where the young feed chiefly on insects, while adult specimens consume fishes. They are mouthbrooders, the female incubating a few large eggs.

There are two other species, the spotted barramundi (*Scleropages leichardtii*), from the Fitzroy River system in Australia, and the northern barramundi (*Scleropages jardinii*), from the rivers of northern Australia and New Guinea. The eggs of *Scleropages leichardtii* are reported to be 10mm(0.4in) in diameter and take 10-14 days to hatch. The fry are 35mm(1.4in) on hatching.

Above: Large shoals of
S. leichardtii, *seen in
public aquariums, are a
grand sight, especially if
viewed in sunlight.*

Left: The large scales of
Scleropages *are highly
attractive, but easily
damaged or dislodged.*

Below: The red form of
S. formosus *is believed
to bring its owner good
luck and is much prized.*

ELECTRIC FISHES

Unique among the vertebrates is the ability of some fishes to produce electricity. Of course, all animals are activated by tiny electrical impulses that spring from nerve endings to muscle cells, but in electric fishes the power of these discharges is amplified in modified muscle tissue called electric organs. When observed through a microscope, a typical electric organ is seen to be composed of a series of disclike modified muscle cells called electroplates, stacked in columns like piles of coins, embedded in a jellylike substance and held together by connective tissue to form a tube. Nerve fibrils connect to one surface of each electroplate and many blood vessels supply the jellylike material. Although the electrical potential of each electroplate is very small, the 'wiring' of the plates in series and the columns in parallel means that a much higher voltage can be produced. The 'design' of the electric organs varies between families and species, but the general principle is the same. Only aquatic creatures could benefit from an electric organ, because water is a much better conductor of electricity than air.

Electric fishes with electric organs can be divided into two groups: those with large electric organs, such as *Malapterurus* and *Electrophorus*, that use them to stun prey as well as to ward off attackers; and those that only produce weaker electrical discharges as a navigational sense. The latter, which include *Gnathonemus* and *Gymnarchus*, have poor vision (interestingly, all electric fishes have small eyes) and live in murky, silt-laden waters. The pulsed electric field they create helps them to orientate and detect other fishes and static objects in the near vicinity. Here, we look at representative examples of both types of electric fishes that can grow to a reasonable size and yet can be kept in an aquarium.

The location of the electric organs

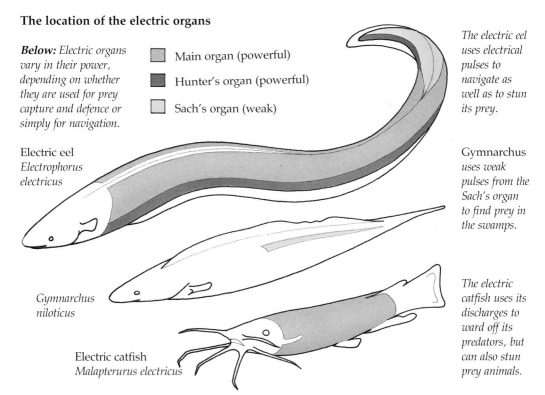

Below: *Electric organs vary in their power, depending on whether they are used for prey capture and defence or simply for navigation.*

- Main organ (powerful)
- Hunter's organ (powerful)
- Sach's organ (weak)

Electric eel
Electrophorus electricus

Gymnarchus
niloticus

Electric catfish
Malapterurus electricus

The electric eel uses electrical pulses to navigate as well as to stun its prey.

Gymnarchus uses weak pulses from the Sach's organ to find prey in the swamps.

The electric catfish uses its discharges to ward off its predators, but can also stun prey animals.

ELECTROPHORUS ELECTRICUS
Electric eel

Size: Up to 2.3m(7.5ft).
Distribution: The Amazon Basin, Brazil,
Guyana, Peru and Venezuela.

The adult electric eel is famed for its ability
to create an electrical discharge of more than
500 volts, powerful enough to stun a horse.
For this reason alone, it is essential to treat
this creature with a great deal of respect
when confining it to an aquarium.

When motionless, the eel is electrically
inert. As it begins to move, however, it
emits short, direction-finding impulses from

*Above: The electric eel
is not particularly
attractive, but is often
displayed in exhibits at*
*public aquariums, where
the electrical discharges it
emits are converted to
sound and/or light.*

the smallest of the three electric organs –
Sachs' organ – situated near the tail. The eel
only becomes dangerous when excited or
frightened; then the remaining two electric
organs may be discharged to deliver a
powerful shock.

Electrophorus electricus is a large and
powerful fish. Adults are olive-brown
overall, with a bright orange throat,
whereas juveniles may be mottled or
banded. The distinctive eyes are emerald

green. Anal and caudal fins are united, but the dorsal and ventral fins are absent.

Young specimens can be readily acclimatized to the aquarium, although they tend to be somewhat quarrelsome among their own kind. Adults are more peaceful. The tank should contain several hiding places among rocks, wood and plants, e.g. the larger *Echinodorus* and *Cryptocoryne* species. Provide subdued lighting and a fine gravel or sand substrate that will not damage the eel's scaleless body.

These nocturnal fishes are seldom seen during daylight hours, but towards dusk they begin to slither around the aquarium in search of food. Feeding them is simple; young specimens thrive on a diet of shrimps, worms, insect larvae and small fishes, whereas adults require large fishes. Live fish can be replaced by pieces of meat or, better still, sprats and similar fish. Electric eels can become tame to the extent that they can be hand fed – with care!

Sex differences are not known, and the only report on brood care was by DuBois-Reymond in 1882, who stated that the young were nursed in the respiratory organ for quite a long time. However, this has not been confirmed and remains doubtful.

GYMNARCHUS NILOTICUS

Size: Up to 90cm(36in).
Distribution: Upper Nile, Chad basin, Senegal to Niger.

This steel-grey to black fish has a long tapering body and a long-based dorsal fin, but lacks ventral, anal and caudal fins. It has a blunt snout with a wide mouth and the short strong teeth are arranged in a single series in both jaws. The electric organ is located on either side of the backbone in the rear half of the body.

G. niloticus is a true carnivore, feeding on small fishes and crustaceans when small and larger prey when adult. In the wild, it inhabits muddy swamps and often hunts at night. In these conditions, the minute eyes are almost useless, and so the fish employs a highly sensitive, though weak, electric field to locate its prey.

Gymnarchus is fascinating to observe in action in the aquarium. It can move backwards or forwards with ease, using

Below: The 'smile' on the face of Gymnarchus niloticus *belies its true predatory nature. In the aquarium it will come to accept most meaty foods.*

Using electricity to locate prey

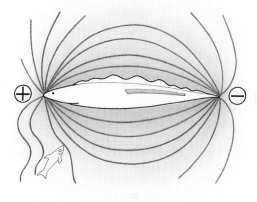

Above: By maintaining an electric field around itself, Gymnarchus *can detect any distortions caused to it as other creatures approach.*

wavelike movements of the dorsal fin, and stalks its prey with minute movements, approaching its victim very slowly. Any evasive movement by the prey is detected as a disturbance of the electric field and compensated for immediately. For the most part, the prey is totally unaware of the presence of *Gymnarchus*.

These fish require shelter and relatively slow water movement in the aquarium. Filtration by external power filter is ideal (if necessary, reduce the power of the return water flow by fitting two spray bars) and regular water changes are beneficial. The water temperature can be within the range 23-30°C(73-86°F), but the fish do best at about 25°C(77°F). Adult specimens are more difficult to acclimatize than juveniles but, once settled, they will happily feed on most meaty foods.

Breeding has only been reported from the wild. About 1,000 amber-coloured eggs, each 10mm(0.4in) in diameter, are laid in a floating nest of plant material and guarded by both parents. On hatching, the fry have long gill filaments and a trailing yolk sac, and surface for air at regular intervals. (In swampy conditions, oxygen levels are low and although they take some dissolved oxygen it is not enough.) The yolk sac is absorbed after about five days and the young leave the nest. At this stage, they are about 5cm(2in) long.

MALAPTERURUS ELECTRICUS
Electric catfish

Size: Up to 65cm(26in).
Distribution: West Africa, Chad, the Nile and central Africa.

The electric catfish has a cylindrical, grey-brown to pinkish body, with numerous darker spots and blotches. The snout is short and wide, the lips fleshy, and the relatively wide mouth is surrounded by three pairs of barbels. The eyes are small and shine like cats' eyes. The dorsal fin is absent and the short, rounded adipose fin is positioned towards the back, close to the caudal fin. The pectoral fins have no spines. The electric organ encases the body of the fish and can be discharged at will. After the first discharge, any rapid subsequent emissions will diminish in power until the fish is able to build up the charge again.

In the aquarium, *Malapterurus* can be encouraged to eat almost anything, but relishes earthworms and meat. Being nocturnal, it is really only suited to the enthusiast who is willing to sit up well into the night to observe it. Electric catfish can be very quarrelsome, particularly with their own kind, and if they bite each other, round sore patches may appear on the body. If the aquarium is to house more than one specimen, be sure to provide sufficient hiding places and separate territories, particularly in the form of caves.

Being sedentary, electric catfishes are susceptible to heater burns. One way to avoid such accidents is to set up an external biological filtration system and install the heating system in this. Alternatively, if the heater remains in the aquarium, surround it with mesh so that the water can flow freely over it, leaving the hot surface out of reach of the fish. Temperatures can be in the range 22-28°C(72-82°F).

There are no reports of captive breeding, which is not altogether surprising, given the natural aggression of these catfishes and the interaction of two electric fields! In the wild, however, females mature at 16cm(6.3in) and breeding appears to coincide with a rise in water levels onto a floodplain.

Two other *Malapterurus* species have been described and there may be a fourth species, as yet undescribed, from the Cameroons. In *Malapterurus microstoma*, the mouth is relatively small, the snout long and narrow and the adipose fin is long and rounded. In *Malapterurus minjiriya*, the mouth and snout are intermediate in shape between *M. electricus* and *M. microstoma*, and the adipose fin is short and slopes back.

Interestingly, *Malapterurus* was known to the ancient Egyptians and appears in hieroglyphics dating from about 4,000 B.C., and in a tomb painting from about 2,750 B.C. Arabs and African peoples also used it to cure ailments by placing it on the affected part of the body, but this practice is not recommended to the hobbyist!

Right: Malapterurus electricus *is not the most endearing creature for the home aquarium, spending most of its time hiding in caves and only emerging to feed. If it senses the presence of live food, it stuns its prey using electricity.*

Below: *The electric catfish is most likely to be observed at dawn and dusk, when it ventures out of its cave in search of food. It is territorial and will protect its territory by whatever means are necessary. Provide hiding places.*

CHARACINS

To date, more than 1,200 species of South American characins have been described, making them one of the largest groups of freshwater fish in South America. They range widely in the Americas, from the Rio Grande in southern Texas through Central America to about latitude 41°S in Argentina. Throughout tropical Africa and in the Nile system, however, there are only some 200 species. The cyprinids are the 'ecological equivalent' of the characins and it is interesting that although the cyprinids occur in Eurasia, the Far East, Australia, Africa and North America, they are absent from South America, where the characins may fulfil the role of the cyprinids. In tropical Africa and the Nile, characins and cyprinids inhabit the same bodies of water.

The characins, in common with the cyprinids and catfishes, possess the Weberian apparatus, a modification of the vertebrae just behind the skull that links the swimbladder to the inner ear. This allows the fish a greater appreciation of both sound and its position in the water column (by detecting changes in water pressure).

Characins have three modified vertebrae linking the swimbladder with the inner ear, whereas in catfishes, the fourth vertebra is also modified. Most characins lack barbels but have teeth in their jaws and the majority have an adipose fin. Thus it is quite easy to distinguish them from the cyprinids.

Characins vary in size from the small *Hyphessobrycon* sp. at 4-5cm (1.6-2in) to *Colossoma* sp., which reach about 1.5cm(5ft) in length. Most characins are omnivorous, opportunistic feeders that take anything from fallen fruit to insect larvae and smaller fishes. The well-known piranha (*Serrasalmus* sp.), on the other hand, is a true carnivore that attacks in shoals and can overcome quite large prey. Other characins are herbivores, whose acute sense of hearing is put to good use during periods of high water when the forests are flooded. They perceive the sound of ripe fruit and nuts falling into the water and congregate in

Below: *Piranhas are often acquired as single specimens and many* *aquarists miss out on the sight of a well-kept shoal in peak condition.*

large shoals to feast on them. Pacu (*Piaractus brachypomum*) are noted for their ability to crack the shells of exceptionally hard nuts to reach the kernels inside.

Most characins require clear, soft, slightly acidic waters with a reasonable flow. In order to maintain these conditions, check that the substrate material and decorative rocks are lime-free. Pieces of bogwood or dead beechwood are a valuable addition to the aquarium, as the tannins they release help to mature the water. Do not allow the pH level to rise too high, however, otherwise the efficiency of the filtration beds will be impaired.

Some species – *Prochilodus* for example – make migratory spawning runs and live in the faster-flowing rivers. In the aquarium, these fish require high oxygen levels and a good flow of water, especially during spells of hot weather when the oxygen-holding capacity of water is decreased.

CHALCEUS MACROLEPIDOTUS
Pink-tailed chalceus

Size: Up to 25cm(10in).
Distribution: Guyana, Surinam, French Guiana and the Amazon Basin.

C. macrolepidotus is a sleek, silver fish with striking pink dorsal, adipose and caudal fins. The leading edges of the ventral and anal fins are also pink and the body is covered with large, easily dislodged scales.

This predatory shoaling fish cruises the upper layers of the water column in search of insects and small fishes. Once acclimatized to aquarium conditions it will thrive, provided there is a good filtration system and a reasonable flow of water. It does not damage plants and is an ideal companion for larger herbivorous catfishes.

The pink-tailed chalceus is an accomplished jumper, so ensure that the aquarium cover glasses are well-fitting. It is also nervous and frightens easily. Floating plants are a useful way of providing cover, but do not allow them to proliferate and so exclude light from other plants.

Feeding *C. macrolepidotus* is easy, as it will accept pieces of meat and fish, and even tablet foods. These fish have been bred successfully in Japan and Hong Kong.

Below: The striking coloration of the pink-tailed chalceus makes it a perennial favourite.

SEMAPROCHILODUS TAENIURUS

Size: Up to 30cm(12in).
Distribution: Amazon Basin.

Semaprochilodus taeniurus is a beautiful shoaling fish for the home aquarium, silvery and deep-bodied, with a characteristic barred caudal fin. A dark band runs along the midline of the body from a point level with the front edge of the dorsal fin into the caudal fin. The dorsal fin has a large dark blotch at its base. The mouth is interesting, as the teeth can be seen on the outermost fringe of the lips, which are pushed forward into a disclike structure when the fish grazes on algae. Indeed, if the algal growth is fairly thick, teeth marks are visible on it after the fish has fed.

S. *taeniurus* is reasonably easy to maintain in the aquarium, given a good flow of well-oxygenated, soft, slightly acidic water in the temperature range 22-26°C(72-79°F). It is a

Above: The mouth of Semaprochilodus taeniurus *is ideally suited to rasping the algae on which it feeds.*

Below: S. taeniurus *is an active shoaling fish that makes an excellent companion for non-predatory catfishes.*

prolific jumper, so the aquarium should have a well-fitting cover. In the wild, *S. taeniurus* undertakes migratory spawning runs, jumping high waterfalls in much the same way as a salmon does in its effort to progress upstream.

Feeding *Semaprochilodus* poses no great problems; as well as accepting peas, spinach and lettuce, they also appreciate small invertebrates, such as *Daphnia*. With regular offerings of *Daphnia*, the body develops much more intense colouring, and shows a metallic sheen when seen in reflected light.

SERRASALMUS NATTERERI
Red piranha

Size: Up to 30cm(12in).
Distribution: The Parana River Basin in South America.

Piranhas have a reputation for attacking in large shoals and stripping the flesh from any creature that enters the rivers they inhabit. This is a somewhat exaggerated claim; it is true that piranhas are voracious carnivores, but they only attack when hungry or cornered. Humans and other animals are not at risk from attack unless they enter the water with a bleeding wound. However, native fishermen do run the risk of losing a finger or a toe when the fish are flapping around in the bottom of their canoes or when they remove the fish from gillnets.

People are attracted to this fish because of its reputation and also because the red piranha is one of the most colourful species. This deep-bodied fish varies in colour, both with age and environmental conditions. Younger specimens are blue-grey along the back, with delicate olive-green flanks and

Below: *If well fed and maintained in good water conditions, the renowned and beautiful piranha will delight its owner for many years. Use plants and bogwood pieces to provide secluded areas.*

Above: Piranha are capable of inflicting fatal damage on fish and can *also mortally wound an injured animal that may fall into the water.*

numerous metallic silvery specks that give the body a spangled appearance. The ventral surfaces, including the pectoral and ventral fins, as far back as the long-based anal fin, are blood-red. The dorsal and caudal fins are dark, but the caudal fin becomes lighter near the caudal peduncle. The anal fin is red with a black margin.

These fishes are unsociable, especially when confined for transportation, and will pick on each other, causing considerable damage to fins and body. It is not uncommon for eyes to be missing from specimens when they are unpacked after shipment. In the aquarium, any companion fish, even if it is the same species, will be bullied if space is limited. However, with sufficient room, piranha do make excellent companions for other large, robust, healthy fishes such as the pimelodid catfishes. When buying piranha, select a shoal of small, young specimens and allow them to grow up together, forming their own hierarchy within the shoal. Provided this is not disturbed by adding more piranha at a later date, the shoal will flourish.

Water conditions are important. These active fishes require high levels of oxygen

and a good flow of water, so external power filters and biological filters are essential. A lime-free gravel substrate is ideal, as the water should be soft and slightly acidic, with a pH level in the region of 6.4-6.8. In harder waters, the fish do not show such intense coloration. Maintain temperatures in the range 24-27°C(75-81°F).

Piranha appreciate sheltered areas in the aquarium, provided by large specimen plants, such as Amazon sword plants (*Echinodorus* sp.), and pieces of bogwood. Although such plants require fairly high lighting levels to maintain growth, their large leaves will provide shaded regions where the fish can feel at ease. To see the red piranha at its best, allow sunlight to fall on the tank. In reflected light, the high-lights and metallic sheens on the flanks of a mature, healthy specimen are magnificent.

Sex differences and breeding behaviour are not known for *Serrasalmus nattereri* (although they are bred by the thousand in Hong Kong), but another species, *Serrasalmus spilopleura*, has been reported to spawn in cichlid fashion, with the male guarding the eggs.

PIARACTUS BRACHYPOMUM
Pacu

Size: Up to 1.5m(5ft).
Distribution: Northern South America.

This deep-bodied, heavily built fish, with its black back and grey belly, is commonly seen in public aquariums but rarely in private collections. It requires a great deal of open water for swimming and prefers to be kept as a shoal. Pacu are vegetarian fishes, living on fruit and seeds in the wild, but they do benefit from some insect larvae and other invertebrates in their diet. In captivity they will eat lettuce, peas, bananas, figs, etc., and they seem particularly fond of small cherry tomatoes, which they eat in one gulp. Being vegetarians, they are relatively inefficient feeders and their waste provides a good nutrient source for some of the detritus sifters, such as the large doradid catfish, *Pseudodoras niger*. However, this accumulation of waste also creates filtration problems. Although large external power

Above: Despite its size, Piaractus is not noted for aggression. Single specimens are usually offered, but it prefers the company of its own kind.

filters can remove the detritus with ease, a biological filterbed system is also required to break it down efficiently. Pacu can tolerate a pH level anywhere between 5.0 and 7.8 and a general hardness in the region of 20°dH. Temperatures should be 22-26°C(72-79°F).

When first introduced, Pacu are very nervous fishes and appreciate the cover afforded by well-established plants. If fed sufficient amounts of green food, they will leave the aquarium decor relatively untouched.

Little is known about the breeding of these creatures and the only known reference to sexual differences relates to another species, *P. mesopotamicus*, in which males have a more pointed dorsal fin than females. Pacu do make migratory spawning runs in large shoals. A similar species, *Colossoma macropomum*, has almost the same distribution and reaches a similar size.

HOPLIAS MALABARICUS
Mud characin

Size: Up to 50cm(20in).
Distribution: Northern and central South America.

Hoplias malabaricus is a specialized predatory characin, armed with a formidable array of teeth. Its mottled, grey-brown body is long and cylindrical, and a broad, dark band runs from the operculum to the base of the caudal fin. This band breaks up as the fish reaches sexual maturity and may vanish altogether with age. The head has several darker bands running down towards the throat, and the fins are brownish with darker spots. There is a black spot at the top of the caudal peduncle. Juveniles are more highly coloured than adults, being dark green to reddish brown dorsally, fading through fawn to pale yellow on the belly. Males are noticeably slimmer than females and their ventral profile is almost straight, whereas that of the female is convex. The

snout of the male is slightly longer and the body is much more intensely coloured.

In the aquarium, this sedentary fish spends much of its time among the plants or resting on pieces of wood, becoming active only during twilight hours. Its coloration enables it to blend easily into the background; indeed, if a substrate of leaf litter is provided, *Hoplias* becomes almost invisible as it lies in wait for passing prey. Once a possible food item has been sighted, a flick of the powerful caudal fin thrusts the fish forward to snap at the unfortunate victim. Should the prey be too large to devour in the initial lunge, *Hoplias* will turn it in its mouth before swallowing it head first. Feeding live fish in the aquarium is unnecessary, unless you wish to observe the hunting habits of the fish. It will relish pieces of fish, meat and prawn, and the addition of the occasional worm is a treat. On such a diet, the growth rate is rapid in the aquarium and one or two days fasting a week is beneficial.

Above: Hoplias malabaricus *spends a great deal of its time concealed among the* *plants and aquarium decor, where it is so well camouflaged that it is almost invisible.*

Breeding has been observed in the wild. In 1919, the fish were seen to mate in pairs and lay eggs over a period of up to 15 days. The eggs were placed in a shallow depression in a sandy substrate from which all the vegetation had been cleared. Later researches in 1942 described *Hoplias malabaricus* nesting in pits in areas of still or slow-moving, shallow water, with a temperature of about 26°C(79°F). These researchers were able to induce spawning by a pituitary injection and described the female cupping her anal fin so that it enveloped the genital orifice of the male, thus retaining the eggs and ensuring their fertilization. The 2mm-diameter(0.08in) adhesive eggs were released into the pit by the female, and guarded by the male until they hatched after 52 hours at 21.5°C(71°F).

DISTICHODUS LUSOSSO

Size: Up to 1m(39in).
Distribution: Zaire Basin.

The reddish ground colour of this long-snouted fish is marked with six to eight dark vertical bars and in juvenile specimens there are darker spots in the dorsal fin. The caudal fin lobes of all *Distichodus* species are partially covered with very small scales.

Distichodus lusosso is predominantly herbivorous, although it will also benefit from vast quantities of live foods, such as *Daphnia*, mosquito larvae and earthworms. If sufficient plant material is provided in the fish's diet, it can be safely housed in a planted aquarium, furnished with, say, tough-leaved Java fern (*Microsorium pteropus*). This plant can also be attached to pieces of wood and rocks, thus providing plenty of shelter for *Distichodus*, which is generally quite nervous and liable to make sudden dashes around the tank if alarmed.

Should they jump, they may well injure themselves on rocks or cover glasses.

Distichodus will tolerate most water conditions that avoid extremes of pH and hardness. Ideally, provide a pH level of 6-7.4 and a general hardness of 10-14°dH. External power filters that create a good flow of water in the aquarium are essential.

Distichodus sexfasciatus is often confused with *Distichodus lusosso* because it has the same general background body colour but with six or seven vertical dark bars and a shorter, blunter snout. Juveniles have a vivid blood red coloration that contrasts with the dark bars. It, too, grows to a length of 1m(39in). A shoal of larger specimens of *D. sexfasciatus* make ideal companions for any fish unable to eat them.

Below: Distichodus lusosso *makes an impressive sight in the large aquarium.*

Right: *With its deeper body and blunt head,* D. sexfasciatus *is often mistaken as* D. lusosso.

CYPRINIDS

The family Cyprinidae has the widest freshwater distribution of any family, with approximately 1,600 species extending from Europe through Asia, Africa and North to Central America. Cyprinids are notably absent from South America, Madagascar, Australia and New Zealand, although man has introduced them in these regions.

In common with the catfishes and characins, cyprinids possess the Weberian apparatus (see page 80). They do not have an adipose fin and some species have barbels around the mouth. There are no teeth in the jaws. Instead, they have pharyngeal teeth, which are absent in the characins. During the breeding season, males of some species develop tubercles on the head, as is clearly seen in *Cyprinus carpio*, the common carp.

Most cyprinids are omnivorous and the majority of the species kept in the aquarium are easy to feed. However, fish is the main food for certain species, whereas others are true herbivores. The latter include *Ctenopharyngodon idella*, the grass carp, which has been used to control water weeds in the USA, Europe and the USSR. Our selection of cyprinids focuses on the larger species

suitable for the hobbyist aquarium.

Within the family Cyprinidae there is a group known in the aquarium trade as 'freshwater sharks', a reference to their streamlined, sharklike appearance, although they are not related in any way to the true marine sharks. The ventral surface is more or less straight, while dorsally the body is arched. The mouth is inferior and may have one or two pairs of barbels. The fins are what everyone expects a fish's fins to look like – well developed and usually held out from the body.

Freshwater sharks are omnivorous. However, a close examination of the mouth reveals ridges and warty growths on the fleshy lips that the fish uses when browsing on algae and plant material, which form the bulk of its diet.

The classic 'freshwater sharks' belong to the genus *Labeo*, and these are widespread in Africa and southern Asia. *Labeo variegatus* is the species featured here.

Below: This small river in Thailand provides a home for many tropical fishes, including a range of cyprinids. Some live in such slow-moving waters, while others thrive in a faster flow.

LABEO VARIEGATUS

Size: Up to 30cm(12in).
Distribution: Zaire Basin, Central Africa.

This is a very attractive member of the genus *Labeo*, but is only infrequently offered for sale. The body shape is typical of the sharks but the attraction of this fish comes from its coloration, both as a juvenile and as an adult. Small specimens, up to about 15cm(6in) long, vary considerably in their coloration, from a creamy yellow background overlaid with a mottled pattern of dark grey to the more highly coloured individuals in which the same basic pattern is embellished with reddish hues on the body and fins. Indeed, it is this variation in the juvenile colour pattern that has given rise to the fish's specific name. As the fish matures, it loses the cream coloration and the body becomes a dark, velvety grey with a red spot on each individual scale. Thus, at all stages of its life, this is an extremely attractive fish.

In captivity, *L. variegatus* will accept a wide variety of foods, including live foods such as *Daphnia*, small freshwater shrimps (*Gammarus* sp.), *Tubifex*, etc., frozen foods and pelleted or flake foods. The water should be soft and slightly acidic, with a temperature range of 22-26°C(72-79°F) and with a good flow rate.

All sharks are active swimmers and *Labeo variegatus* is no exception. It requires a large aquarium with plenty of room to move. Sharp objects should be avoided as the large scales are easily dislodged. Provide cover in the form of thickets of plants and, although *L. variegatus* will graze on the leaves, the plants should not suffer if you offer sufficient plant material in the diet. Without this seclusion in the aquarium, the fish are prone to leaping from the water when frightened and can easily damage themselves. Not surprisingly, well-fitting cover glasses are essential.

Although not aggressive, *L. variegatus* can be fairly quarrelsome among its own kind. If you attempt to keep several specimens together, watch for any signs of bullying. If the aquarium is large enough – at least 2mx60cmx60cm(79x24x24in) – it is easier to raise two or three small specimens to maturity and have them accept each other than to attempt to introduce another individual into an already established community of fishes.

Often confused with *L. variegatus* is *Labeo congoro*. This fish also comes from the Zaire Basin, but the main difference is that

Below: Labeo variegatus *is aptly named; this youngster will gradually lose its* variegated pattern and become an impressive velvety black adult, with a red spot on each scale.

juveniles have the adult coloration of a grey black body with a red spot on each scale and this pattern does not change as they mature. They grow a little larger than *L. variegatus*, reaching about 40cm(16in), but their care in the aquarium is the same.

Little is known about the breeding behaviour of either *L. variegatus* or *L. congoro*.

BALANTIOCHEILUS MELANOPTERUS
Silver shark; Bala shark

Size: Up to 35cm(14in).
Distribution: Thailand, Malayan Peninsula and Sumatra.

As its common name suggests, *Balantiocheilus melanopterus* has a silver body. In contrast to this, all the fins (except the pectorals, which are clear) are yellow with deep, black margins. This combination produces a very attractive aquarium fish.

Silver sharks are gregarious creatures that prefer to be kept in shoals of six or more and, although they do not grow to a great size, they flourish in a large aquarium with plenty of open space for swimming. They are also prolific jumpers, so a tight-fitting cover glass is essential. Tank decoration is a matter of personal choice, but vine roots

Above: Provide areas of open water for the fast-swimming silver shark. A shoal will provide movement and interest in the show aquarium.

and well-established specimens of *Cryptocoryne* sp. and *Echinodorus* sp. seem to suit them very well. Avoid rocks, as silver sharks are easily frightened and may dislodge scales if they dash against them. Although happy in a brightly lit aquarium, these fish are seen to their best advantage in natural sunlight.

To maintain silver sharks in their optimum colours and condition it is important to provide suitable water conditions and correct feeding. The water should be soft and slightly acidic - about 6°dH and pH 6.5-7.0. Silver sharks like highly oxygenated, clear water with a good flow. This can be achieved by using an undertank biological filter, the water being returned to the main aquarium via a powerful pump. They need a varied diet that includes *Daphnia*, *Tubifex*, and mosquito larvae (preferably live but frozen is accepted), flake foods, and vegetable matter such as lettuce and peas.

Silver sharks are very peaceful and make excellent companions for some of the larger, placid catfishes such as *Pseudodoras niger*. Alternatively, they can be kept with some of the other large cyprinids. Nothing is known about their breeding habits.

BARBUS SCHWANENFELDI
Tinfoil barb

Size: Up to 35cm(14in).
Distribution: Southeast Asia, Thailand, Malay Peninsula, Borneo, Sumatra.

The deep silver body of this very attractive fish has golden overtones, while the dorsal fin is red with a black tip and the caudal fin is red with black bars on the outer edge of both lobes. The remaining fins are red-orange, but in young specimens the fins appear yellow rather than red. There are two pairs of barbels around the mouth.

Barbus schwanenfeldi is very active, requiring plenty of space and highly oxygenated, soft and slightly acidic water in the temperature range of 21-24°C(70-75°F). Lighting should be sufficient for good plant growth, but provide shaded areas as well. Aquarium plants are best sited towards the sides and rear of the aquarium and, to avoid them being eaten by the tinfoils, provide the fish with plenty of vegetable matter in their diet. They will accept other foods and, indeed, if they are to achieve high coloration with a really silvery sheen on the body, they will need a very varied diet that includes live foods, such as *Daphnia*, *Tubifex* worms and mosquito larvae, as well as good-quality flake foods. They will also take small fishes if the opportunity arises. Growth is rapid if the fish are well fed.

Inexperienced aquarists who buy tinfoil barbs because of their striking appearance are disappointed when they very soon outgrow the community tank. However, in a large aquarium (2mx1mx60cm deep/79x39x24in), a shoal of six or eight of these peaceful free-swimming fishes would make an excellent choice to accompany more sedentary species, such as catfish or the more peaceful cichlids.

Below: Given good aquarium conditions, tinfoil barbs will grow from small, poorly coloured individuals into resplendent fishes.

LABIOBARBUS BURMANICUS

Size: Up to 30cm(12in).
Distribution: Burma, Thailand.

A dark spot on each scale gives the impression of dark longitudinal bars following the rows of scales along the silvery body of *Labiobarbus burmanicus*. The body shape is similar to that of most *Labeo* species, but instead of the short-based dorsal fin of *Labeo*, *Labiobarbus* has a long-based dorsal fin, with the first rays noticeably longer than the rest.

In the aquarium, this very peaceful fish spends much of its time browsing on the algae that grows on plants and wood, but these activities cause little or no damage to the plants. It also accepts flake foods and smaller live foods (*Daphnia*, *Tubifex*, etc.), as well as peas and lettuce. Use an external power filter to provide a good flow of water through the aquarium. This fish will grow well in clear, well-oxygenated water that avoids extremes of pH and hardness.

***Below:** Labiobarbus burmanicus is an enthusiastic herbivore, grazing on fast-growing* *Java moss and helping the fishkeeper by keeping this invasive plant under control in the aquarium.*

LEPTOBARBUS HOEVENII

Size: Up to 50cm(20in).
Distribution: Sumatra, Borneo, Thailand.

The body of this exceedingly beautiful, streamlined fish has a metallic sheen, greenish gold along the back, shading to green and finally silver along the belly. The dorsal and pectoral fins are clear, while the ventral, anal and caudal fins are reddish. There is a black spot behind the gill and these fish have two pairs of barbels. Juveniles have a dark line running along the midline of the body from the head to the base of the caudal fin, but this line breaks up and finally disappears with age.

Leptobarbus hoevenii is a very active fish, fond of jumping and swimming against a current. A good flow of water is, therefore, essential, so provide a powerful external filter, as well as a biological undertank system to keep the water in prime condition. The water should not be too hard, say 12°dH general hardness, and neutral (pH value of 7.0). Temperatures in the range 21-25°C(70-77°F) are suitable. *Leptobarbus hoevenii* will take most dried and frozen foods, but it prefers live food, if available, supplemented with peas.

Above: *These lively young specimens of* Leptobarbus hoevenii *will soon grow into elegant, streamlined adults if given sufficient space in which to swim.*

Right: *Thickly wooded hills surround this fast-flowing river in Borneo. Such waters form the ideal habitat for* Leptobarbus hoevenii *and other shoaling fishes.*

These are shoaling, river fish and should be kept in groups, even in the aquarium. Juveniles settle down quickly within the confines of an aquarium and are peaceful. If they are startled, however, they may crash wildly around the aquarium, dislodging scales and leaving themselves open to fungal infections. (Tackle these promptly – see page 44.) In Thailand, this fish is a favourite among anglers, as it puts up quite a fight when hooked, taking any bait from prawn to vegetation. It is not highly prized as a food fish; indeed, at certain times of the year the flesh is said to be poisonous.

CATFISHES

Catfishes (Siluriformes) form the second largest order of primary freshwater fishes, i.e. those that originated from freshwater ancestry. Indeed, catfishes have existed for a very long time; *Silurus*, for example, has been recorded from the Eocene epoch (approximately 55-38 million years ago). Today, there are 33 families of catfish, with more than 2,000 species widely distributed across the world. Two families have secondarily migrated to a marine existence: the Ariidae and Plotosidae.

In common with the cyprinids (barbs, labeos, etc.) cobitids (loaches), gymnarchid eels and the characins, all catfishes possess the Weberian apparatus, a mechanism that links the swimbladder to the inner ear by means of modifications to the first four vertebrae of the backbone. This enables the fish to gain a better perception of their position in the water column and also allows a greater sensitivity to sound and vibration. Some catfishes are capable of using atmospheric air as an accessory means of respiration in low-oxygen conditions.

Above: Catfishes can flourish in such murky waters, here in Sri Lanka, using their barbels to locate food in the gloomy conditions.

Below: Most catfishes, such as this Clarias, seek out secluded areas of the aquarium. They can be seen resting at most times of the day.

Left: Barbels come in many different forms. This Sorubim lima *has simple, unbranched barbels – one pair situated above the mouth (maxillary) and two pairs located below the mouth (mandibular).*

Below: Although the maxillary barbels of this Synodontis *are simple, the mandibular barbels are branched, which provides a greater area for taste reception when hunting for prey items.*

All catfishes have barbels – whiskerlike appendages near the mouth – from which they derive their common name. The number and size of the barbels can vary greatly, from a single pair in *Ageniosus* sp. to 24 pairs in *Aspredinichthys tibicen*. They are covered by taste sensors used in the search for food. There are basically three types of barbels: maxillary, mandibular and nasal, reflecting their position on the head.

The maxillary barbels, positioned above the mouth, are usually the most prominent and can be extremely long. In some of the pimelodids and bagrids, the modified maxillary bone extends into the base of the maxillary barbels, making them highly manoeuvrable. When used for hunting, they are held forward so that the fish can 'taste' the water. As one barbel approaches a possible prey item, the other moves slowly to join it, until the catfish has determined the exact position of the food fish and can lunge forward to despatch its unwary victim.

The mandibular barbels are situated below the mouth, so that the fish can sense what is underneath it. Many catfish swim with their mandibular barbels barely touching the substrate, but as soon as they contact a likely source of food they dig into the sand. In the mochokids and some doradids, these barbels have become branched, giving a greater surface area to otherwise short barbels. The nasal barbels are located on top of the head, close to the

nostrils. They are normally short, but perform the same tasting function as the other barbels. (In catfishes with a single pair of barbels, these are usually maxillary.)

The catfish skull is covered by a thin layer of skin and the various bony projections can be a useful guide to determining species. Catfishes do not have scales, but in some genera, including *Scoloplax*, *Sorubim* and *Phractura*, bony dermal plates develop from folds in the skin and slowly ossify. These plates are most apparent in the South American families. The Doradidae have a single row of bony plates with backwardly projecting scutes along the midline of the body; the Callichthyidae have two rows of plates that meet at the midline of the body; and the Loricariidae have three rows of plates, an upper, mid and lower series.

Catfishes can use their stout dorsal and pectoral fin spines in self-defence, locking them in the extended position and effectively increasing their body size, which makes it very difficult for a prospective predator to swallow them. Sometimes, the spines are serrated and can cause very nasty, painful wounds should one become stuck in the hand or arm of an unwary fishkeeper. The pimelodids and clariids are notorious in this respect; although the wound appears trivial at first, it soon begins to throb and swell, until often it is impossible to bend the affected limb for up to 24 hours. Hospital treatment may be required. Other catfish species, including *Heteropneustes fossilis* and the plotosids, can excrete a poison from the base of the pectoral spine. The ultimate defence/hunting mechanism is found in the electric catfish, *Malapterurus electricus* from Africa, which can discharge a strong electric current (see page 78 for more details).

Catfishes in general are difficult, if not impossible, to sex. However, with more mature specimens, it may be possible to distinguish males by the fleshy growths on the head (as in some loricariids), by slight differences in ventral fin shape (as in *Corydoras*), by genital papillae (as in some bagrids) or by a thickening of the pectoral fin spine (as can be seen in *Callichthys* and *Hoplosternum*). Others may exhibit subtle changes in fin shape (some ariids), or body shape (most species). Experienced aquarists

Above: *The Doradidae have heavy armouring on the body. The scutes are sharp and can inflict painful wounds. Be sure to handle with care!*

can discern these slight differences between the sexes. Breeding strategies vary: *Callichthys* species are bubblenest builders; some of the clariids and doradids are nest builders; but some of the loricariids simply place their eggs on leaves, rocks or submerged tree roots. In all these catfishes, the male guards the eggs, but the ariids incubate their eggs in the mouth, whereas aspridinid eggs are carried on the belly of the female. Yet other catfishes, the schilbeids, for example, do not practice any parental care at all and merely scatter their eggs among plants.

The following selection includes some of the largest and most spectacular species.

ICTALURUS PUNCTATUS
Spotted or channel catfish

Size: Up to 110cm(43in).
Distribution: Southern and southwestern USA. Also widely introduced as a sport fish in Europe.

The channel catfish is a long slim fish with a depressed head, four pairs of barbels, and quite large laterally placed eyes. The colour is very variable, ranging from light brown to a darker grey-green dorsally, with the belly fawn to white. There is sometimes a scattering of small, dark spots on the flanks. The fins are usually clear but sometimes

have a darker edge. The caudal fin is deeply forked. Juvenile specimens are most often offered for sale and these are attractively marked, but these spots gradually fade as the fish matures. Albino specimens are also available. These have the typical albino coloration of creamy white tinged with pink on the body and creamy white to clear fins; the eyes may be either pink or black.

In the aquarium, try to avoid the temperature rising above 15°C(59F°); in warmer water the oxygen levels drop and the fish show signs of distress, such as gasping at the surface. This can be alleviated in the short term by increasing the water flow through the aquarium, boosting the aeration and adding ice blocks to reduce the temperature. Make the ice blocks in 1-litre ice-cream tubs and, ideally, use water from the aquarium. This will avoid adding too much 'new' water to the system, should a heatwave continue for any length of time.

The channel catfish will tolerate a wide range of water conditions, flourishing in a pH range of 6.0-8.0 and a general hardness range of 4-30°dH. Make sure that the aquarium is filtered with a biological filter capable of dealing with the copious amounts of waste products from the fish. Predominantly a predator, *Ictalurus punctatus* will consume just about anything offered to it, from pieces of meat or fish and earthworms to high-protein pelleted foods.

A gravel substrate is best for this fish, as it will continually dig through a finer medium and cloud the water. Any plants should be hardy species such as Java fern or Amazon swords; alternatively, use plastic plants. Keep the lighting subdued and create hiding places with pieces of bogwood. If you prefer rocks as tank decoration then be sure to avoid any that have sharp, jagged edges; the naked body of the channel catfish is easily damaged.

This coldwater species will happily adapt to pond conditions. It is often sold as a scavenger for ponds, but very few people appreciate the size it can ultimately attain or, indeed, the number of small goldfish or koi it can, and will, consume.

It is possible to breed *Ictalurus punctatus*, but this can only be accomplished in a pond or very large aquarium, such as the tanks in a public aquarium. The fish pair and dig a depression in the substrate. Here, the female lays clumps of eggs that are then guarded by the male. Channel catfish are highly prized as a food fish in the USA and are farmed commercially in several states.

Below: Ictalurus punctatus *is one of the few catfish available to the hobbyist as an albino and in its normal brown to grey-green coloration.*

PSEUDODORAS NIGER

Size: Up to 84cm(33in).
Distribution: The Amazon Basin.

The body and fins of *Pseudodoras niger* are a uniform black to slate grey, fading to a lighter grey on the belly. In juveniles, the coloration is more mottled, but this becomes less distinct once the fish is about 10cm(4in) long. The body is covered with a thick, warty skin and a single row of narrow, lateral plates runs from behind the head to the caudal peduncle. All but the first three of these plates have a single backwardly projecting scute. The snout is conical with an inferior mouth.

In the wild, *Pseudodoras niger* feeds on insect larvae, plant material, fruits and general detritus, which it sifts from the sand and mud. In the roof and floor of the fish's mouth are several fleshy appendages, covered in taste receptors. These are an extension of the sensory apparatus of the barbels, and act like a tongue when the fish is sifting for food. This method of feeding can be used to great advantage in the aquarium if these catfishes are introduced as companions to some of the larger vegetarian fishes, such as *Piaractus* species, whose

Above: Pseudodoras niger *is a gentle giant, ideal for aquarists who do not wish to keep the more quarrelsome fishes.*

Below: Note the fleshy appendages covered with taste receptors located inside the mouth of Pseudodoras niger.

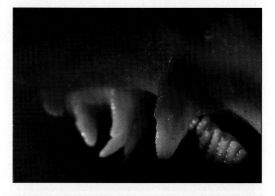

nutrient-rich droppings form an important source of nourishment (see page 84 for further details). *P. niger* also consumes vast quantities of pelleted food.

Pseudodoras prefer a temperature range of 21-26°C(70-79°F). Being fairly active swimmers, they require plenty of oxygen in the water and this can be supplied by a powerful external power filter with a spraybar return. Avoid extremes of hardness and maintain the pH level within the range 6.0-7.6 for best results.

In the aquarium, this catfish can be classed as a gentle giant, showing no aggressive tendencies towards its companions. Small specimens are timid and spend much of the time hidden away, only venturing out to feed in the twilight hours, but as they mature, they cruise around the aquarium more boldly. Despite their propensity for sifting through the substrate, they will not dislodge well-rooted plants such as *Echinodorus* and *Cryptocoryne* species; indeed, young specimens acclimatize far more quickly in a well-planted community aquarium than in a relatively bare aquarium full of larger fish.

MEGALODORAS IRWINI

Size: Up to 60cm(24in).
Distribution: Brazilian Amazon, Rio Maranon (Peru), Guyana, Surinam and French Guiana.

The body coloration is basically light brown with large, dark brown, irregular blotches; the belly is more mottled, with the darker colour predominating. All fins have dark brown or black spots except for the long, low adipose fin, which is light brown on the keel and darker at the base.

The body is heavily armoured with a single row of 15-18 bony plates along the flanks. Each of these plates has a formidable backwardly projecting scute capable of inflicting painful wounds. Since the fin spines are also very well developed, it is advisable to treat this creature with a great deal of respect when trying to move it from one one aquarium to another. If given the opportunity, the fish will trap your fingers between its pectoral fin and its body, which in itself is a painful enough experience but, not satisfied with this, it then swiftly swings the caudal fin round, inflicting deep lacerations on the trapped hand with the scutes on the body plates.

Young specimens adapt easily to aquarium conditions, especially if they are initially introduced into a well-established, planted tank. Youngsters will feed on frozen bloodworms, smaller pelleted foods, and live foods such as *Daphnia* and *Tubifex*. As the fish grows, offer progressively larger items of food, such as earthworms, pieces of meat and aquatic snails. In fact, *Megalodoras irwini* has a great liking for snails and will consume these avidly. In the wild, snails

Below: Megalodoras irwini *is slow-growing and relatively peaceful. It adapts to aquarium life and benefits from snails as part of the diet. Keep the tank water stable, clean and well-filtered.*

form such a large part of the diet of these fish that the Creole Indian name for them means 'mother of snails'. In captivity, small apple snails (*Ampularia* sp.) fill this gap in their diet and are greedily consumed.

Provide clear, well-oxygenated water for *Megalodoras* by using a suitable external power filter. Avoid extremes of pH and hardness values and maintain the temperature in the range 22-25°C(72-77°F). This slow-growing doradid is a welcome addition to the larger aquarium, being peaceful and attractive. It is most active at dawn and dusk, when more mature specimens can be observed feeding; young specimens are more secretive in their habits. Take care not to house juvenile *Megalodoras* with fishes that it can swallow; it is not a voracious predator, but is not averse to eating smaller fishes.

Below: Although not as striking as L. pictus, Leiarius marmoratus *is attractively patterned and requires the same aquarium care. Monitor water conditions in the tank to avoid the risk of damage to the fish.*

Right: Long barbels are a main feature of the predatory Leiarius pictus. *Provide plenty of swimming space in the tank; if it is unable to move the barbels freely as it searches for food, it becomes nervous.*

LEIARIUS PICTUS

Size: Up to 60cm(24in).
Distribution: The upper Amazon River and its tributaries.

This very striking member of the Pimelodidae has a dark brown body with darker spots and a light-coloured belly. Two pale cream bands extend along the body, the first from the base of the dorsal spine down towards the ventral fin and then along the lower body to the caudal fin. The second, much finer band, begins at the base of the third to sixth soft rays of the dorsal fin and runs parallel to the first in the upper part of the body. The sail-like dorsal, adipose and caudal fins have much larger dark spots than the anal and ventral fins. In adults, the caudal fin is deeply forked with

pointed lobes; in young specimens, these lobes are rounded. There are three pairs of banded barbels. These become shorter in relation to body length in adult specimens; in juveniles, the maxillary barbels extend well beyond the tips of the caudal fin, whereas in adults they reach just beyond the dorsal fin.

Leiarius pictus needs plenty of tank space to move around in and sufficient room to extend its long maxillary barbels above and in front of it as it searches for food. If the barbels touch the sides of the aquarium, the fish will become very agitated, dashing wildly around and damaging itself. *Leiarius* is a piscivore and often fails to settle in the confines of an aquarium unless fed live fishes. However, given time, it is possible to change its diet to dead fish and meat, tablet and frozen foods.

In the wild, these large pimelodids are found near rapids in deeper rivers, where there is a high oxygen level in the water. In captivity, it is important to maintain good water conditions, as any build-up of nitrites will quickly affect the fish, resulting in degeneration of the barbels and the membrane between the fin rays. Combine mechanical filtration, using an external power filter with a high flow rate, a biological filter system and regular partial water changes for the best results. The pH level should be 6.5-7.5 and water hardness in the range of 10-18°dH.

Although *Leiarius pictus* is highly territorial, it makes an excellent companion for large characins and cichlids, as well as for other catfishes in a spacious tank.

PHRACTOCEPHALUS HEMIOLIOPTERUS
Redtailed catfish

Size: To 1.5m(5ft).
Distribution: The Amazon and Orinoco Basins.

This large, heavily built pimelodid has a very characteristic colour pattern. The head is light grey with dark spots, each one smaller than the diameter of the eye, and the upper part of the body is dark grey to black, while the lower half is white with a dark grey to black band extending from the pectoral to the ventral fin. This band may be absent on some specimens. The dorsal and adipose fins are dark grey with a yellow-orange margin, and the caudal fin is red. The anal and ventral fins are grey and sometimes have a yellow-orange margin, while only the leading edge of the pectoral fin spine is orange, the remainder being grey. Coloration is very variable, especially between juveniles and mature specimens. Juveniles have a spot on either side of the dorsal fin. Research shows that there are two colour variations of the caudal fin – pink and red. Even if shrimps and colour enhancers are fed to the pink-tailed form, the caudal fin does not become red. This suggests that distinct populations occur, but a great deal of field research would be required to determine this.

In the wild, these creatures are reported to feed on crabs and other crustaceans, but in captivity they appear to eat just about anything, from strips of white fish to earthworms. The smaller the specimen, the smaller the food offered to it should be. Do not be tempted to overfeed *Phractocephalus*; being predators, they benefit from periods of fasting. In any case, if the belly is rounded after feeding, allow this to return to normal before offering more food.

Redtailed catfish are prone to shedding the body mucus, especially when under stress, the mucus being seen as a mass drifting through the aquarium. In young specimens, gasping at the surface, swimbladder problems and degeneration of the barbels are indicative of nitrite and ammonia problems, and a highly efficient, mature biological filtration system is essential to maintain water quality. In the short term, commercial preparations are available to deal with potentially dangerous ammonia and nitrite levels in the aquarium, but these are designed for emergency use and are not intended to replace an efficient filtration system.

Phractocephalus are very sensitive to water changes, so never replace more than 10 percent of their water at any one time. Aerate the replacement water and allow it to stand for 24 hours before adding it to the tank, but if this is not possible, use a

dechlorinating agent instead. These fish
prefer alkaline water, with a pH level of
7.2-7.6, and temperatures in the range 21-
27°C(70-81°F), but remember that the higher
the temperature, the better the aeration
system will need to be. (At higher
temperatures, the water contains less
dissolved oxygen, but since the fish's
metabolism speeds up, it is more active and
therefore requires more oxygen to function.)

This fish requires as much space as
possible. Juveniles may be quarrelsome and
very territorial so, unless you have an
extremely large tank, it is better to keep a
single specimen. Aquarium decoration will
vary; small specimens need plants and
caves in which to hide, whereas adults will
destroy your carefully designed aquarium
with one flick of the tail. In a tank housing a
larger specimen, it is better to provide one
or two large pieces of wood or rock,
anchored on the bottom glass of the tank,
thus allowing more room for the fish to
swim. Once settled in the aquarium, a
redtailed catfish will become hand tame.

SORUBIM LIMA
Shovelnose catfish

Size: Up to 60cm(24in).
Distribution: The Amazon River, and rivers
in Venezuela and Paraguay.

Sorubim lima is the most commonly available
shovelnose catfish. It is very distinctive,
with one dark band along the top of the
body and another along the flanks,
beginning at the snout and continuing into
the lower lobe of the caudal fin. The lower
flanks and belly are silvery white and there
is a series of small dermal plates on the
front portion of the lateral line. In juvenile
specimens, the upper lobe of the caudal fin
is larger than the lower.

This catfish thrives in a planted aquarium,
where it can hide in wait for prey or hunt
among the stems of tall growing plants. It is
most active at night. It does not appear to
quarrel with its own kind and will share the
tank with other inhabitants as long as they
are large enough not to be eaten.

Shovelnose catfish appreciate live fish,
but can just as easily be fed live prawns and

Above: *The redtailed
catfish has shot to fame
over the last few years,
and many small
specimens have been
imported. Given
favourable conditions and
food items of a suitable
size, they will grow into
magnificent specimens.
However, take care not
to overfeed them.*

Right: Sorubim lima *is
considered to be one of
the more commonly
available catfishes. It
adapts well to a captive
existence and makes an
ideal subject for the home
aquarium. A group of
shovelnose catfishes will
do well when kept as a
group in the tank and do
not quarrel.*

earthworms to accustom them to life in the
aquarium. Later, this diet can be changed to
dead meaty foods and tablet foods.

Water conditions are not critical; a pH
level of 6.5-7.5 and a hardness of up to
20°dH are acceptable. Filtration should be
via an external power filter or biological
filter. As with *Leiarius* and *Pseudoplatystoma*,
any deterioration in water quality will
become apparent by the degeneration of the
barbels and fin membranes. And in
common with *Phractocephalus*, this fish has a
further indicator of distress; it frequently
sheds the mucus from the body.

PSEUDOPLATYSTOMA FASCIATUM
Tiger shovelnose

Size: In excess of 1.5m(5ft).
Distribution: Northern and eastern South America, east of the Andes, south to the Parana – La Plata Basin.

The large, predatory shovelnose catfish is another fish with long barbels that needs a tank of sufficient length and width to accommodate it. If unable to move its barbels freely, a 50cm(20in) specimen has been known to take fright and punch its way through the end panel of an aquarium measuring 2x1x1m(79x39x39in).

This sleek, streamlined fish has a silvery grey body shading to a darker olive along the back, the underside being creamy white. The markings are very variable, but usually appear as vertical dark stripes or blotches. The finnage is spotted and the caudal fin deeply forked. The head is long and depressed, with the upper jaw longer than the lower. There are three pairs of barbels – one maxillary and two mandibulary pairs.

Pseudoplatystoma fasciatum inhabits large

Left: The tiger shovel-nose is a large predator that lurks beneath pieces of wood before lunging at passing prey. Provide a large tank for the fish to swim without damaging its sensitive barbels.

Above: This juvenile Sorubimichthys planiceps *is typical of specimens on sale and retains its coloration as an adult. Pay careful attention to the water conditions in the tank.*

rivers and the deeper sections of smaller rivers. The stomach contents of specimens from the Rio Jiparana in western Brazil showed that these voracious predators had been feeding on small loricariids, freshwater crabs, an anostomid characin and a cichlid. In the aquarium, the fish can be fed twice a week on a diet of trout, sprats, prawns and similar foods.

The natives consider these fish to be excellent food, particularly when the firm flesh is fried or grilled. Naturally, when large specimens are caught they are killed for the pot rather than exported for the aquarium trade. Maintenance requirements in the aquarium are generally the same as for any other large pimelodid – an excellent filtration system, highly oxygenated water, regular water changes and a temperature of about 22°C(72°F). *P. fasciatum* will tolerate a wide pH range of 6.0-8.0 and also a wide general hardness range of 4-30°dH.

SORUBIMICHTHYS PLANICEPS

Size: Over 2m(6ft 7in).
Distribution: The Amazon and Orinoco rivers and their tributaries.

This magnificent catfish has an extremely large head and a long sinuous body, culminating in a large, deeply forked caudal fin. The back and head are grey-brown and covered with numerous small dark spots. There is a midlateral white band, bordered by two dark brown stripes that extend into the upper and lower lobes of the caudal fin. The belly is white, sometimes marked with small spots.

No matter how well fed it is, the elongated body of this piscivorous fish always makes it appear emaciated. Given a very large aquarium, with plenty of plants and hiding places so that it can hunt for its prey, it adapts well to life in captivity, feeding on strips of fish, pelleted foods and earthworms.

Filtration should be via an external power filter combined with a biological filter. Being fairly active, *S. planiceps* requires a high oxygen content in the water. It is sensitive to the water conditions and requires soft, slightly acidic water with a pH of 6.5-7.0 and a maximum of 18°dH general hardness.

PSEUDOHEMIODON LATICEPS
Whiptail catfish

Size: Up to 30cm(12in).
Distribution: The Orinoco Basin.

Although no giant among aquarium fishes, the whiptail catfish makes an ideal companion for other large fishes. Its body is depressed, covered with bony plates and light tan in colour. The head and body are covered with small, dark spots that form radiating lines on the head and transverse lines on the body. The lips are heavily fringed, but the lower surface of the head is naked. The upper caudal lobe is extended into a long filament, which has prompted its common name.

Pseudohemiodon requires a very fine substrate, as it spends much of its time buried in the sand. When feeding, it filters sand through the gills in search of any insect larvae or detritus. A diet of *Tubifex*, *Daphnia* and green food will keep it in good condition. The whiptail catfish appreciates a good flow of water in the aquarium and a temperature range of 22-27°C(72-81°F). Maintain the pH level in the range of 6.4-7.0 and a water hardness of 10-18°dH.

Breeding details are scarce, but observations made in the wild mention adults carrying 5mm(0.2in) diameter eggs and on hatching the fry were approximately 16mm(0.6in) in length, excluding the caudal fin. The heads of the newly hatched fry were seen to be much more rounded than those of the adults and the filament on the upper lobe of the caudal fin was already prominent at this stage.

PTERYGOPLICHTHYS GIBBICEPS

Size: Up to 50cm(20in).
Distribution: Orinoco and Amazon Basins.

This very spectacular loricariid has a dark brown body with large black spots – a colour pattern that extends into all the fins. The caudal fin has an orange-brown margin and the leading edges of the pectoral fins are similarly coloured. The dorsal fin is long-based, and in juvenile specimens appears sail-like and extremely large in comparison to the body length.

In their natural habitat, *P. gibbiceps* often browse on the algae growing on rocks and submerged branches in the shallow, brightly lit regions of the river. To prevent damage to the retina in these bright conditions, loricariids have developed a retractable lobe that partially covers the iris, acting as a sunshade. Under dim conditions, however, the lobe is completely

Left: P. laticeps *has an unusual mouth with fringed lips. The fish is reported to carry its tiny eggs on these lips.*

Above: P. laticeps *spends much of its time buried in the fine sandy substrate, so that only its eyes are visible.*

retracted, allowing the fish to take full advantage of all the available light.

In the wild, this catfish occurs in shoals. In the aquarium it can be territorial, but if the tank is sufficiently large, with plenty of hiding places or dense plant cover, it is possible to keep several specimens together. They are not aggressive towards other fishes and make excellent companions in a community of large fishes.

Feeding is not a problem, as *P. gibbiceps* is vegetarian and will consume large quantities of algae. In the evening, they can often be observed browsing on the algae attached to plant leaves and, providing there is enough algae, the fish will not harm the plants. Additional substitute foods can take the form of lettuce, frozen peas and pelleted food.

Being a herbivore, this fish excretes heavily and puts a considerable strain on the filtration system, but a large-volume power filter, combined with a biological filter, should be able to cope. In nature, they graze in clear waters near rapids and

Above: P. gibbiceps *has long been a firm favourite with aquarists. Unfortunately, the magnificent sail-like fin of this juvenile will not grow in proportion with the rest of the body.*

among riffles, where the water is highly oxygenated. A power filter will not only help to recreate this habitat, but the added water movement at the surface will also boost the oxygen content. *Pterygoplichthys gibbiceps* can tolerate a wide range of pH (6.5-7.8) and hardness levels (4-20°dH), and will thrive at 22-26°C(72-79°F).

Little is known about the breeding habits of this fish, nor is it possible to readily distinguish the sexes. However, they are bred commercially in Singapore.

Another species commonly found in the aquarium hobby, *Pterygoplichthys annisitsi*, is known to excavate burrows in the river banks. During the dry season, it is found curled up in these holes, well above the water level, remaining there until the rains return and the rivers flood. This fish is a welcome addition to the home aquarium.

SILURUS GLANIS
European wels

Size: Up to 3m(almost 10ft).
Distribution: Central and eastern Europe, southern regions of the USSR, including the basins of the Black, Caspian and Aral Seas.

Silurus glanis is the only true European catfish and has been of commercial importance to man for many decades, being widely farmed, and fished by rod and line or traps. This large fish can weigh up to 200kg(440lb) when fully grown and is generally caught at about 2m(6ft 7in) long. The largest recorded specimen, caught in the River Dnepr (flowing through the Ukraine into the Black Sea) was measured at 5m(16ft 5in) long and weighed 306kg(675lb). The flesh, especially near the caudal peduncle, is white, fatty and palatable, and in northern Europe it is dried and the fat used as lard.

The European wels is an unprepossessing fish, dark grey (including the fins) and sometimes marbled or marked with spots or blotches. Albino and semi-albino specimens have occasionally been caught, mostly in eastern Europe. The head is depressed and the wide mouth has three pairs of barbels. The maxillary barbels are particularly long,

extending beyond the pectoral fins when laid back along the body. The dorsal fin is small and there is no adipose fin. The anal fin is long-based.

These fish do very well in an unheated aquarium or garden pool, but note that small specimens are easier to acclimatize to aquarium conditions than semi-adults, which are more set in their feeding patterns. They will eat anything and everything and initial growth is rapid, as might be expected from a fish that can grow up to 3m(10ft) long. In the wild, juveniles eat small fishes and invertebrates; as they mature, they take large fish, waterfowl and even, on occasion, small mammals.

In the aquarium, the main problem is cleanliness. *Silurus glanis* are notoriously filthy creatures, feeding heavily and therefore producing a large amount of waste. Furthermore, they have a habit of stirring up the substrate with one flick of their caudal fin, giving the tank a very cloudy appearance. A powerful and efficient filtration system, provided by a large external power filter combined with undertank filter beds, is essential to keep this fish in perfect condition. In addition, carry out regular partial water changes of up to 30 percent every 10 days.

The chances of spawning this fish in the aquarium are remote. In the wild, they breed during May and June in shallow, weedy areas near the banks of rivers and lakes. About 100,000 green, adhesive eggs, 2-3mm(about 0.01in) in diameter, are laid on plants and guarded by the male. They hatch within 16-19 days and the fry, closely resembling black tadpoles, grow rapidly.

Above: *Coming across a large specimen of* Silurus glanis *on its own territory is enough to give anyone a fright. It can grow to a length of almost 3m(10ft).*

Left: *Even in a tank, the wels catfish will soon attain a reasonable size. If kept in the garden pond, it flourishes on a diet of koi and goldfish.*

Right: *Occasionally you may find an albino form of* Siluris glanis, *but these are not readily available through the trade. The fish's normal colour is dark grey.*

AUCHENOGLANIS OCCIDENTALIS
Giraffe catfish

Size: Up to 50cm(20in).
Distribution: Widespread throughout Africa.

The coloration of *Auchenoglanis occidentalis* can be variable. The fish may be a uniform dark to pale brown, with a creamy white belly or the base colour may be overlaid with a latticework of pale lines, resembling the colour patterning on a giraffe, hence its common name. This pattern may or may not spread into the finnage. The long pointed snout of this fairly thickset catfish is adorned with three pairs of barbels.

Giraffe catfish can be observed sifting through the substrate in search of worms and detritus, and grow rapidly on a diet of live foods, such as *Tubifex*, *Daphnia*, insect larvae, nymphs and earthworms. Dried foods, especially the tablet varieties, are eagerly accepted, as are small amounts of vegetable matter, such as peas.

Above: *The giraffe catfish is a sociable and unassuming detritus feeder, whose only vice is to rearrange the fine substrate when feeding.*

Below: *This lovely marbled patterning on young specimens of A. occidentalis has given rise to their common name – giraffe catfish.*

Set up the aquarium with a relatively powerful filtration system, an external power filter to create a good flow of water and a trickle filter. Water conditions should be slightly soft and acidic, with a temperature range of 22-28°C(72-82°F). A fine, sandy substrate is good for these fishes because it does not damage the barbels when they are feeding. Small specimens are ideal for the home aquarium and make excellent companions for larger midwater swimming fishes. Although unrelated, the giraffe catfish has a similar lifestyle to *Pseudodoras niger* (see page 98).

CHANNALLABES APUS

Size: Up to 30cm(12in).
Distribution: Angola and the Zaire Basin.

This catfish could easily be mistaken for an aquatic snake. The dorsal, caudal and anal fins are united; the pectoral fins are greatly reduced and the ventral fins are absent. The body is a uniform dark brown.

This unusual member of the family Clariidae is able to breathe atmospheric air.

Above: This member of the Clariidae family, Channallabes apus, is not as boisterous as many of the better known Clarias species.

When kept in the aquarium, it will be seen to take gulps of air at the surface at regular intervals. It is a great escape artist and will get out through the smallest aperture, so ensure that the aquarium is well covered. It is undemanding to keep, feeding being a simple matter as the fish will accept most prepared pelleted foods as well as pieces of meat, larger insect larvae and, if the opportunity arises, live fish. It is tolerant of most water conditions, except extremes of pH and hardness.

Channallabes tends to bury itself in the substrate, and filtration sand provides it with an ideal opportunity to do so without fear of damaging its naked body. Remove any mulm and debris disturbed by this activity by using an efficient external power filter. *Channallabes* prefers a secluded aquarium with overhanging roots and thickets of plants. The roots of the plants also serve to bind the substrate together and prevent the catfish from causing too much disturbance in the aquarium.

BAGRICHTHYS HYPSELEOPTERUS
Black lancer

Size: Up to 40cm(16in).
Distribution: Palembang, Sumatra.

The name 'black lancer' derives from the elongated dorsal spine of the adult fishes, but the hobbyist looking through a dealer's tanks will probably only find a small black fish that, depending on size, may have a white lateral stripe. At this stage, the dorsal spine extends only marginally above the fin membrane. The colour is velvety black, with a lateral white band. The body shape changes as the fish grows: whereas the head profile is almost straight in juveniles, in adults it steepens and becomes concave. In juveniles, the first few rays of the upper lobe of the forked caudal fin are abbreviated, giving the appearance of malformation. This feature gradually disappears, until the adults display a deeply forked caudal fin, with filamentous extensions on both lobes. There are four pair of barbels.

To see adult *Bagrichthys hypseleopterus* swimming with the dorsal fin fully erected, it is vital to house it in a deep aquarium. This timid fish prefers to remain in secluded areas of the aquarium, except when feeding. The black lancer appreciates earthworms

Above: The dorsal fin spine of this juvenile black lancer will become more elongated as the fish matures. The body shape will also alter.

Below: Mystus nemurus *is one of the most sought-after bagrids because of its striking coloration, which develops as it matures.*

and pelleted foods, but it is a good idea to offer a variety of tempting morsels when acclimatizing the fish. Although good filtration is required, the water flow in the aquarium need not be excessive; *Bagrichthys* tends to shy away from the water flow and seek out more tranquil areas.

MYSTUS NEMURUS

Size: Up to 60cm(24in).
Distribution: Thailand, the Malay Peninsula, Sumatra and Java.

Mystus nemurus is one catfish whose colour improves with age. As juveniles, about 15cm(6in) long, they are drab, grey-black fishes, with white flashes on the hard rays of the caudal fin. Once the fish reaches a length of 45-60cm(18-24in), the body colour changes to steel blue, the caudal fin becomes red and the barbels are white. When frightened or provoked, the white barbels turn black almost instantly.

This predatory catfish uses its long barbels in much the same way as the pimelodids of South America, for hunting in murky waters. Feeding *Mystus nemurus* poses no problems – it will consume anything it can get into its rather large mouth, from pieces of fish to the fingers of the unwary aquarist! It is a vicious fish, best kept alone, but housing can be a problem, as they have a habit of jumping and will even penetrate a 10mm(0.4in) thick cover glass weighted down with bricks. Ideally, the aquarium should be covered with an unbreakable material, such as wood. Floating plants have a beneficial effect, as they give the fish a sense of security.

In the wild, this fish is found in both freshwater and brackish water environments. In the aquarium, *Mystus nemurus* tolerates most water conditions, showing none of the barbel and fin membrane deterioration evident in South American pimelodids when a water change is overdue. It appears to do best in harder, alkaline waters in the temperature range 22-25°C(72-77°F). Although *Mystus nemurus* will survive in less than optimum conditions, good filtration via an external power filter and biological filter is nevertheless important because a build-up of nitrites or ammonia could cause problems.

CLARIAS BATRACHUS
Walking catfish

Size: Up to 55cm(22in).
Distribution: Eastern India, Sri Lanka, Burma, Thailand, the Malay Peninsula and Sumatra.

Clarias batrachus is a member of the Clariidae, a family which has a very wide distribution. In Africa, they are represented by *Channallabes*, *Heterobranchus*, and *Gymnallabes*, as well as several species of the genus *Clarias*. *Clarias batrachus* extends the range of the family into Asia.

All members of the Clariidae are characterized by an elongate, naked body, broad depressed head, large mouth and four pairs of barbels – one nasal pair, one maxillary pair and two mandibular pairs. Perhaps they are best known for their ability to use atmospheric air while crossing marshy areas, hunting for food, or just surviving in very poorly oxygenated waters. The accessory air-breathing organs are spongelike structures, situated behind the gills in an extension to the gill chamber. Clariids have also been known to bury themselves in mud for days in an attempt to survive when rivers, lakes and waterholes dry up. This need for atmospheric air means that clariids will often make rapid dashes up to the surface to gulp in air.

Clarias batrachus is the most commonly available species, dark brown in colour with numerous white spots and a lighter underside. The base colour continues into the long-based dorsal and anal fins. In males, the dorsal fin has darker spots with a larger black blotch towards the rear of the fin, whereas females have no dark markings in the dorsal fin and the general coloration is not so intense. The commercially bred albino version is frequently seen.

Clarias batrachus is probably one of the easiest fishes to keep in captivity and will eat just about anything, from live fish, worms, pieces of fish and meat to vegetable matter, such as brussel sprouts, pieces of fruit and softened rolled oats. Often, they will gorge themselves to such an extent that they appear to have swallowed a golf ball; if this happens, allow several days to elapse before feeding again.

Just because they tolerate most water conditions and are generally regarded as almost indestructible, it would be wrong simply to put these fish in an aquarium and leave them to fend for themselves. They appreciate a soft substrate in which they can root around for tasty morsels and will take advantage of the security offered by hiding places among rocks and wood. Although they enjoy excavating the substrate, well-rooted, established plants will remain untouched. Despite their ability to survive in stagnant, oxygen-deficient waters, it is important to keep the aquarium water well filtered, using a biological filter and an external power filter to remove the large amounts of waste these creatures produce.

A tight-fitting cover on the aquarium is equally important, as *Clarias* in general have achieved great notoriety as escape artists. One notable example – a 30cm(12in) specimen confined to a 60x30x30cm (24x12x12in) aquarium during a three-day exhibition – easily shattered a 6mm(0.25in) wire-reinforced plate glass cover, held in place by several house bricks, on the first night. Following much turmoil, as it tried to bite the exhibition stewards attempting to catch it, it was only confined to quarters when a second aquarium was placed on top of the first and half-filled with water! This specimen had once before been found covered in dust and dog hairs under the seat of the car on the way to another exhibition and, on another occasion, in a semi-desiccated condition on the floor of the fish room when a cover glass was not properly replaced. Its cantankerous nature also extended to biting the hand that fed it while cleaning the aquarium. Needless to say, it lived alone.

As soon as *Clarias batrachus* is introduced into the aquarium, its natural predatory behaviour becomes apparent, especially if the tank contains fishes small enough to fit into its mouth. If several juveniles are confined in a relatively small tank, they will show cannibalistic tendencies. They are also highly territorial – even moving a single rock in the aquarium can set up boundary disputes, sometimes resulting in the death of one of the protagonists.

There has been much research into the breeding of *Clarias* species. Reports show that *Clarias batrachus* spawns in rice fields, where it constructs a nest among the submerged vegetation in which to deposit its adhesive eggs. These are then guarded by the male. This species has also been observed making holes 20cm(8in) in

diameter and 25cm(10in) deep in the banks of a watercourse, just below the surface, and depositing eggs inside. Between 2,000 and 15,000 fry were reared in each hole.

In *Clarias mossambicus*, artifically fertilized 2mm(0.08in) diameter adhesive eggs took 24-30 hours to hatch. Other reports reveal that 1.5mm(0.06in) eggs with a large adhesive disc hatched within 23-25 hours at a temperature of 22-28°C(72-82°F). The young appeared in groups of between 5 and 11 individuals. Work on the spawning behaviour and early development of *Clarias gariepinnus* shows that it spawns at night, usually after heavy rains. Large numbers of fish gather together and the males fight before courtship begins. Spawning takes place in shallow water among submerged vegetation, but the parents do not protect their young. The fry are capable of swimming strongly only 48 hours after hatching and feed on the small invertebrates that abound in the shallows.

Clarias has been widely introduced into developing countries as a food fish, generally to the detriment of native fishes, as the *Clarias* escape from fish farms and decimate the local fish populations.

Above: *Such albino specimens of* Clarias batrachus *are more often available than the standard species below.*

Below: Clarias *are great escapers, but are able to survive for many hours, provided they do not dry out completely.*

SWAMP EELS

These are not true eels, but members of the family Synbranchidae. They are found in tropical fresh and brackish waters of America, Africa and Asia through the Indo-Australian archipelago to the Australian mainland. The dorsal and anal fins are greatly reduced, have no fin rays and run as ridges along the top and bottom of the body to join with the caudal fin, which may have 8-10 rays. The pectoral and ventral fins are lacking. A single slit on the underside of the head is the gill opening.

Synbranchids are able to breathe air, which they take in by gulping at the surface. The oxygen is absorbed when the air is held in the gill pouch or passed through the hind portion of the gut. This feature allows swamp eels to live in slow-moving or stagnant bodies of water and, should conditions deteriorate to the extent that the watercourse dries up, the swamp eel will burrow into the mud and aestivate. Some species also migrate overland in search of new watercourses.

SYNBRANCHUS MARMORATUS

Size: Up to 1.5m(5ft).
Distribution: Southern Mexico to Argentina. Also reported from Cuba.

The coloration of this typically eel-shaped fish is variable, but it is usually dark brown with darker spots and blotches, and a lighter belly.

Young specimens adapt well to aquarium life. They like a soft, sandy substrate in which they can bury themselves and copious amounts of food in the form of worms and insect larvae. Once established, they will feed on pieces of meat, prawn and

Below: This savanna pond in East Africa is typical of the stagnant waters in which swamp eels thrive. They can aestivate in droughts.

Above: Synbranchus marmoratus *is a great escape artist. Tight-* *fitting cover glasses are essential for maximum security and warmth.*

fish, but rarely accept tablet foods. As they get older, they become somewhat quarrelsome and are best kept on their own. Take care when cleaning the aquarium, as the fish may attack your hands.

The water temperature should be in the region of 25-28°C(77-82°F), as these creatures seem to thrive in warmer conditions. A tight-fitting cover glass not only ensures that they remain in the aquarium, but also that they take in warm and not cold air at the water surface. An external power filter is sufficient to maintain the swamp eels in good condition.

The ability to retain air in its extensible gill chamber allows *Synbranchus marmoratus* to travel for long distances over land. Should it escape from the aquarium, it will survive for a long time, provided the room temperature is not too low. A shrivelled specimen found on the floor should always be returned to the water, in case there is still a spark of life. During the dry season, *Synbranchus marmoratus* buries itself in the mud. When the rains arrive, the natives fish for it in the main river channels.

SIAMESE TIGERFISH

The Siamese tigerfish must not be confused with the Siamese fighting fish, an unrelated species. In the family Lobotidae there are four species of *Datnioides*. Here we consider the commonly known *D. microlepis* and *D. quadrifasciatus*. The body is compressed and very deep, and the lateral line is arched and complete. The anterior part of the dorsal fin is composed of spines, the posterior portion of soft rays. The jaws are protractile.

DATNIOIDES MICROLEPIS

Size: Up to 50cm(20in).
Distribution: Cambodia, Thailand, Sumatra and Borneo.

The background coloration of this fish varies from a clear creamy white to pale tan, with six or seven vertical jet black bars. The number of black bars depends on geographical location: fish from the Asiatic mainland have six bars, whereas those from the Indo-Australian archipelago have seven. These bars do not converge with age. The lateral line has 105 scales and the dorsal fin shows 15 or 16 soft branched rays.

Datnioides microlepis adapts easily to aquarium conditions and several fish can be kept together. The tank should be planted with large-leaved plants, such as *Cryptocoryne*, as *D. microlepis* likes to lurk beneath the leaves. (See page 37 for more details on these plants.) Its swimming movements are usually slow and deliberate, especially when stalking prey. As it approaches a shrimp or small fish, the Siamese tiger very slowly sways from side to side, as if sighting the prey. Then it edges forward and engulfs the food. It is not necessary to feed live foods to *Datnioides microlepis*, as it will accept pieces of meat and fish. Even so, its growth rate is slow.

Siamese tigers prefer hard, alkaline water that is well filtered and clear. While *D. quadrifasciatus* will only thrive in brackish water (see below), personal experience has

Above: When feeding, the jaws of Datnioides *extend forward to engulf quite large prey items.*

Below: D. microlepis *flourishes in fresh water, but looks as if it belongs in a marine aquarium.*

Above: *As a juvenile,*
D. microlepis *has very*
distinct cream and black
vertical bars. With age,

the colours become rather
drab, with the cream
colour having an almost
'dirty' appearance.

shown that *D. microlepis* flourishes in fresh water. When buying *D. microlepis*, try to find out what type of water they were imported in and, if brackish, acclimatize them slowly to fresh water.

In Thailand, *D. microlepis* is sought after as a food fish, as the flesh is reported to have an excellent flavour.

DATNIOIDES QUADRIFASCIATUS

Size: Up to 40cm(16in).
Distribution: The Ganges River to Burma, Thailand, Malaya, the Indo-Australian Archipelago.

This fish differs from *Datnioides microlepis* in having only 70 scales in the lateral line and 13 or 14 soft branched rays in the dorsal fin. The body has 8-10 vertical black bars, some of which converge as the fish ages, and the intervening bars are silvery white. There is a black spot on the operculum.

Datnioides quadrifasciatus requires brackish water to thrive and is far more difficult to acclimatize to aquarium conditions than *Datnioides microlepis*. A voracious predator, it eats mostly live foods, such as shrimps, insect larvae and fishes.

CICHLIDS

Cichlids are a very diverse group of fishes. In terms of global distribution, they are widespread, being found on three continents – America, Africa and Asia. There is enormous variation in size; the smallest dwarf cichlids grow to only 5cm(2in), whereas *Boulengerochromis* sp. and some *Cichlasoma* sp. may reach well over 60cm(24in). Some cichlids live in still pools, others at the bottom of waterfalls. Among the larger cichlids, behavioural patterns differ greatly. Some are highly predatory, while others are almost scavengers or, at best, opportunistic feeders, making a meal of whatever comes their way. Others may be specialist feeders, obtaining the bulk of their nutritional needs by feeding on one particular food, such as snails or, in one case, the eyes of other fishes.

Staking territory
All large cichlids are territorial, some more so than others and there is good reason why this is such an integral part of a cichlid's behaviour. These fish often live in highly populated waters and, if they are to breed and rear offspring to maturity, they need to establish a piece of territory that most other fish will fear to enter. This allows the fry to establish themselves and gives them a greater chance of reaching adulthood. If a cichlid can establish a large enough area of its own, it will be less aggressive. The fewer the number of cichlids in a tank, the less aggression they are likely to display, but only a cichlid knows how much space it wants. Often, one intruder will be allowed to enter a cichlid's territory, whereas another will be violently expelled.

Cichlids may stake their territory in one of several ways, and once these are understood it is easier for the aquarist to reduce their annoying effects. Firstly – and most importantly – a male cichlid will display increased aggression when spawning. Having secured a female, he will guard her jealously. Any other cichlid – or any other fish, for that matter – that resembles another male will be regarded as a threat and becomes the victim of aggressive blows to the flanks and fins. If this behaviour is allowed to continue unchecked, the victim will eventually find itself trapped in one upper corner of the aquarium, and left to die with its fins destroyed. To guard against such outbursts, ensure that the mix of cichlids in the aquarium varies in shape, colour, size and behaviour. The greater the diversity of inmates, the better the chance of success, but cichlids are very individual and a lack of aggression can never be guaranteed.

The best combination of cichlids is probably two different opportunist feeders, one piscivore and one or two species that are a mix between the two, along with, say, two or three catfish. (This amounts to seven or eight fish. As a guide, up to eight 25-30cm(10-12in) fish could live comfortably in a 680 litre(150 gallon) tank. In a smaller aquarium, reduce the number or size of fish accordingly.) Quite a number of fishes will mix with cichlids. Most large catfish do well in a cichlid aquarium, once they have discovered that it is safest to stay away from a given territory. Tinfoil barbs (*Barbus schwanenfeldi*) often make good tankmates and it is very surprising how many

Below: *These fry of a pair of* Cichlasoma synspilum *will remain* carefully concealed in a rocky cave for about five days before surfacing.

medium-sized, non-cichlid species can be kept with the non-piscivorous cichlids.

In order to stake out territory, a cichlid likes to leave physical markers. Often, it will dig into the gravel and excavate a large hole with huge mounds on the outskirts. Any fish venturing near such a construction knows immediately that something of significance created it and that it forms a territorial marker; it enters at its peril! Unfortunately, there are always some cichlids that will simply not tolerate others and these fishes must be kept on their own. This applies mainly to the largest piscivores. Another solution is to crowd an aquarium with so many fish that any aggression is diluted by the weight of numbers, but this is hardly the kindest way to keep cichlids.

Furnishing the aquarium

A fish on the losing end of a fight needs to find a safe haven and to help it the fishkeeper can employ some subtle tricks. In most cases, but not always, it is the smaller fish that are subjected to bullying. By creating caves that are only large enough to accommodate these smaller fish, you are providing them with their own safety zone. Flowerpots and clay pipes, available from a building supply company, are ideal refuges for the smaller tank occupants, but bear in mind that these fish will grow and flowerpots may need replacing with larger ones at a later date for them to be effective.

Above: A river in East Africa, where cichlids and other fishes must adapt to changing water levels and conditions throughout the year.

Most aquarists prefer to use some form of undergravel filtration and the constant digging of cichlids can render these partially inactive. It is a good idea, therefore, to incorporate some form of barrier in the middle of the substrate to prevent the undergravel plates being exposed and the filter breached. So-called 'gravel tidies' make a good barrier for cichlids; strong nylon mesh will stop all but the most determined cichlid from reaching the bottom. Gravel tidies do have one slight disadvantage, however. If a pair of cichlids spawn and place their newly hatched fry onto a gravel tidy, these are likely to fall through the holes and be lost. If you wish to encourage spawning, it is probably better to use fine net curtain as a substrate barrier, but this is more difficult to keep in place, since it tends to float.

Obviously, plants are unlikely to thrive if the cichlids are constantly digging up the aquarium gravel. Most cichlid keepers decorate their aquariums without plants and achieve some stunning aquascapes using plenty of large pieces of rock, built up to form great contours with large fissures. Tuffa, sandstone and limestone make good-quality building materials, but due to their somewhat soluble composition they are really only appropriate for Rift Valley species or Central American species that will tolerate a water hardness of 15°dH or more. Where species require somewhat softer or acidic water, then consider using rock such as slate, granite or basalt.

If you feel you must have plants in the aquarium, then plastic ones are probably the best option. There are various ways of preventing them from being uprooted. Probably the least satisfactory method is to place the plastic plants into the gravel and surround the base with pieces of slate in order to stop the fishes digging near them. A better method is to remove the base of a large clay flowerpot so that you are left with something resembling a large terracotta 'washer'. Remove the foliage of the plastic plant from its base, push it through the flowerpot washer and then reassemble the plant. This gives the plant a much heavier, larger base and a greater chance of staying in place. The third method, and undoubtedly the best, is to glue the plastic plants to a large piece of glass with some silicone aquarium sealant. When dry, place the plant in the aquarium and cover the glass with gravel. This is the most cichlid-proof method, but remember that a small patch of the undergravel filter underneath the glass may not be functioning as efficiently as it could.

Lighting the aquarium
It is natural to assume that because a cichlid is large, boisterous and aggressive, it is obviously not shy, but this is not the case. Virtually all cichlids are shy and retiring to some degree, although some may be much more shy than others. Lighting is the single most important factor in persuading a cichlid to settle down in a new aquarium. Unless you intend to include live plants in the aquarium, all you require is sufficient light to view the fishes comfortably. Grolux lighting is the most complimentary to a cichlid's colours and the 'softest' of the available wavelengths. About 30 watts of Grolux lighting over an aquarium with a capacity of 270 litres(60 gallons) is usually ample. Cichlids are much more prone to be timid and jumpy in an aquarium which is overlit rather than underlit, particularly the Central American species.

Filtration for cichlids
Cichlids are highly susceptible to contaminants in the water, and if they are to thrive in captivity they must have very clean conditions. In their native waters, cichlids may be injured by aggressors and predators, but they generally recover by dint of their natural resistance and with the assistance of nature. In an aquarium, we create a false environment in which the fish population is probably higher than in the wild and the water retains a greater number of waste products. In these conditions, the nitrate level soon increases, leading to nitrite and, eventually, even ammonia poisoning, with fatal consequences. Therefore, a good filtration system is a necessity. It is practically impossible to over-filter a cichlid aquarium, and most cichlid keepers use a combination of two filter systems – an undergravel biological filter and an external mechanical filter. Undergravel filters in conjunction with gravel tidies are the ideal foundation of a good biological filtration system for cichlids, especially if you add a powerhead (an electrically driven water pump fitted on the top of the uplift tube) to produce a greater water flow through the system. During their industrious excavating activities, cichlids throw up a great deal of large particulate waste. A mechanical filter, such as an external canister filter, will help keep the water clear and also reduces the amount of waste loading the biological system.

When cichlids are kept in less than ideal conditions, they are far more prone to disease. Finrot, fungus, ulcers and hole-in-the-head disease are all direct or indirect consequences of poor water quality. In order to maintain the cichlid's environment at its optimum level, carry out large-volume water changes on a weekly basis, or preferably twice weekly. A 40 percent water change twice a week is not an uncommon procedure and, if carried out regularly, will encourage large cichlids to thrive.

Feeding
It is important to understand the basic feeding pattern of any cichlid that you intend to introduce into your aquarium. They may be herbivores, piscivores, omnivores or micropredators. While many

come to accept an 'unnatural' food, such as beef heart, providing a near natural diet during the first week or two will help to make the initial introduction to a new aquarium much more successful. In particular, predatory cichlids, such as the wolf cichlid (*Cichlasoma dovii*), are much easier to establish if fed with small dead fish or, better still, with live food, such as deformed or surplus fry from another cichlid spawning. It is not uncommon to encourage a particularly prolific pair of cichlids to breed in order to provide live food for a large predatory cichlid, young cichlids often being the food for larger fishes in their natural environments.

Once established in their aquarium, cichlids usually take all manner of foods, such as beef heart (blended), raw fish, prawns, pelleted and flaked foods, whitebait, woodlice, earthworms, small snails, runt fish, garden peas and sweet corn; in fact, many cichlids are virtually waste bins with fins!

General care
Finally, a couple of points about protecting large cichlids. These fishes are often too aggressive for their own good and it is sensible to take a couple of precautions. For example, heater-thermostats may be bitten

Above: Cichlasoma managuense *and other large cichlids create a* lot of waste. Good *filtration is essential for them to reach full size.*

or slapped by a powerful tail, leading to breakages and potential disaster, so wrap them loosely in some form of plastic garden mesh. Another cichlid pastime is to leap from an uncovered tank and flip about on the floor. Keep the tank covered at all times, using cover glasses that are thicker than 6mm(about 0.25in); anything less substantial may be dislodged or broken by these heavy, powerful fishes. Never put your hand near a large parental cichlid, since they defend their fry avidly and are not afraid to bite.

On the following pages, you will find more detailed descriptions of several large cichlid species, many of which will live together in relative harmony, as long as you choose their tankmates with care. All will thrive in ordinary tap water at 27°C(81°F), unless otherwise stated.

Always remember that everything in the large cichlid aquarium is a compromise: a compromise between the number of fish, the number of caves and the amount of space. It takes time to find the right compromise, but once achieved, the rewards are phenomenal.

SOUTH AMERICAN CICHLIDS

AEQUIDENS SPECIES *CF. RIVULATUS*
Green terror

Size: Up to 28cm(11in).
Distribution: It is impossible to give an accurate guide to its origins, although the 'silver edge' is reputed to come from Peru and the 'gold edge' from Ecuador.

There is some confusion over this species. Originally, the fish found in the hobby was nothing more than a large blue acara (*Aequidens pulcher*), but green in colour, with a silvery white edge to the dorsal fin. In the mid-1980s, it became apparent that the common name 'green terror' was being used to describe a very different fish. This one grew much larger, had a very powerful head, and was brilliant green in colour, with a bright orange-gold edge to the dorsal fin.

Above: *Although very aggressive to males of the same species, this 'silver edge' green terror is relatively easy to spawn. Provide a varied diet.*

Below: *The vivid colour of the dorsal fin makes the 'gold edge' the slightly more popular of the two known forms of this cichlid species.*

When kept in the same tank, these fishes became increasingly intolerant of each other as they grew, particularly of other males. To confuse matters even more, specimens of this fish began to appear with a bright silver edge to the dorsal fin. Today, the original smaller fish is believed to be *Aequidens rivulatus* and the two latter fish are usually referred to as *Aequidens* species *cf. rivulatus*, with the addition of either 'gold edge' or 'silver edge', depending on the colour in the dorsal fin. (The German word 'Saum' may be used instead of 'edge'). This is the true green terror, the silver and gold edges to the fins being regional variations.

The coloration of this fish is quite magnificent. The broad and powerful head has a base olive colour, but the cheeks have many green to blue lines, squiggles and spots, and the lips are bright green. The scales on the flanks are bright green with a black blotch on the trailing edges, making them look very geometric in shape. The green coloration becomes even more intense in the fins, verging towards blue. All the fin markings are formed by intricate lines and spots. The centre of the body has a black spot, typically seen in cichlids. Males are distinguishable from females by their more powerful, solid heads and longer, more pointed fins. The coloration in the dorsal fin is usually less intense in females.

This species is by no means as aggressive as its intimidating name might suggest, at least not as far as other fishes of other species are concerned. However, 'terror' may strike where more than one adult male of the same species is kept in the same tank. These fish are highly territorial and males will fight continuously for sovereignty of a given area. Females tend to be spared, as long as they are willing to cooperate when the male's urge to spawn prevails. If she is an unwilling partner at this time, then her life may be in peril.

If kept by itself, pampered on a varied menu and given abundant water changes, the green terror grows almost 28cm(11in) long. It will eat all manner of foods, especially earthworms, beef heart, food pellets, bloodworm and woodlice. Do not feed the same food continuously, as this can lead to an 'addiction' to one food and digestive disorders.

Despite its reputation for aggression, this is one of the easier South American cichlids to induce into spawning. Males will court females by exhibiting a great deal, 'fluttering' with their fins while excavating a large pit and biting at a potential spawning site. The pair are open breeders, selecting a flat stone or similar medium on which to lay their eggs. Both fish care for the eggs and fry, although the female usually carries out the majority of the parental duties.

ASTRONOTUS OCELLATUS
Oscar; marble cichlid; velvet cichlid

Size: Up to 38cm(15in).
Distribution: The Oscar originates from South America, in particular Brazil, and is found in many tributaries of both the Amazon and Orinoco river systems. It has been released into the rivers and lakes of Florida, where it thrives. Here, fishermen find it a great sporting fish and call it the peacock, or tail-eyed, bass.

The Oscar must be the best-known and most popular of all the larger cichlids. Its body is very deep and thick, the fins are rounded and the very broad caudal peduncle powers the fish through the water towards its prey. The large mouth has thick lips and the eyes are large and protruding.

The original wild form has fairly uninteresting coloration, although its marbled pattern of olive and brown is undoubtedly interesting. The only true colour found on the body is a bright orange or red ocellus, or eye-spot, on the caudal peduncle and, sometimes, at the base of the dorsal fin. In captivity, this fish has been selectively bred to produce several other 'morphs', or 'colour sports'. Some have red coloration covering approximately 50 percent of the body and are known as red tiger oscars, while those with red scales covering nearly the whole of the body are usually called red oscars. In recent years, oscars with greatly extended finnage have been developed and given the name long-finned oscar, but these seem to be less popular than their original counterparts.

Sexing this fish by sight is nearly impossible. The most effective way is to

feed the fish well and increase the water temperature. This usually induces the spawning tubes to drop slightly, the male's being narrow and pointed while the female's is shorter and blunter. The easiest way to establish a pair is to place five or six juveniles together in an aquarium and let them pair off naturally as they mature.

Given ideal conditions, oscars can grow to a total length of over 38cm(15in). A large aquarium, measuring at least 120x45x45cm (48x18x18in) is essential, as are frequent large water changes. Unfortunately, this fish has the most appalling feeding habits. Any food being chewed in the mouth is usually spewed out through the gills, creating all manner of mess. It is vital, therefore, to install an extremely efficient biological filtration system and a mechanical filter is a valuable addition.

In the wild, oscars live in slow-moving backwaters and pools where the waters are very clean and warm, often approaching 30°C(86°F). They are highly predatory,

Above: The oscar is the most popular of the large cichlids kept in the aquarium. Greed and a constant awareness of the world outside the tank are two of its most endearing features.

living almost entirely on the smaller fishes and insect life that share their rivers. However, in captivity, oscars are quick to realize that life can be easier and they soon adapt to feeding on anything that their owner is kind enough to throw into the tank. Earthworms, snails and woodlice all make good live foods. More conveniently, beef heart, raw fish, whitebait, prawns and food pellets are all taken with a crazed rush to the surface.

Oscars often spawn in capativity, provided they have a sufficiently large tank with a capacity of 360 litres(79 gallons) or more. (As a guide, a tank measuring 120cm long, 45cm wide and 75cm deep/48x18x30in will hold about 360 litres.) The pair select an open site and deposit 1,500 eggs or more on a piece of rock. The pair guard and fan the eggs for three days until they hatch and for a further five days until the young are free swimming in the aquarium.

This is one of the least aggressive of all the larger cichlids available today. Although the oscar can be quite intolerant of its own kind, it rarely pursues a vendetta with another species for any length of time. It is easily tamed, often learning to distinguish its owner from strangers and very willing to feed straight from the hand.

HOPLARCHUS PSITTACUS
Parrot cichlid; false mouth cichlid

Size: Up to 30cm(12in).
Distribution: Brazil, but quite restricted, being found in the upper Rio Negro.

Whether this cichlid derives its first common from its parrotlike face or its parrot-green body coloration is uncertain. Unfortunately, parrot cichlids are not seen in the hobby as often as they should be. In juvenile fishes, the body pattern is very interesting. A long band of blotches runs the length of the body from the eye to the caudal peduncle, where there is a small round spot. The rest of the body is covered in a very complicated mottled camouflage pattern of light and dark grey, which affords considerable protection from predators. As it grows, the body colour changes from grey to an intense green. The head becomes more solid and the iris of the eye develops a red hue. One notable marking is a line that runs from the eye to just above the mouth, which accounts for the cichlid's other common name of 'false mouth cichlid'.

A suitable diet for the parrot cichlid would include some live food, along with some form of vegetable matter, such as tinned garden peas (with the skins removed) or sweet corn.

Parrot cichlids are very exacting as far as water composition is concerned. Although young and adult fish will tolerate hard or medium-hard water, they will not really thrive unless their water is soft and slightly acidic (with a general hardness of about

Below: The parrot cichlid is one of the less common large South American cichlids. Its nervous character makes it a challenge to spawn. It is vital to provide clean water for this species to flourish in the home aquarium.

8°dH and a pH value of 6.4-6.7). They will certainly not spawn unless these conditions are provided. Even low levels of metabolic waste in the aquarium will quickly lead to a loss of appetite and eventual ill-health. When small, these fish are very nervous, shoaling together quite tightly and hiding in any rocky crevice. They remain quite timid, with a tendency to take fright easily, which often leads to sudden fits of panic, with the fish rushing haphazardly around the tank and crashing into the decor. Providing a secure environment with plastic plants and pieces of bogwood for cover will help the fish to settle down. Optimum water conditions and very low lighting levels also help to ease the situation.

Suitable tankmates for this fish include severums (*Heros severus*), waroos (*Uaru amphiacanthoides*) and festivums (*Mesonauta festivus*). All these fish require similar water conditions and share the same timid disposition. The parrot cichlid is far from aggressive and will usually only do battle with fellow males of its own species.

Pieces of slate arranged in a vertical formation make suitable spawning sites. These cichlids lay about 800 eggs on this smooth surface and guard them for a week. Once the fry are free swimming, feed them with newly hatched brineshrimp. They may also obtain some nourishment by feeding from the parental mucus in a similar fashion to discus (*Symphysodon*).

CENTRAL AMERICAN CICHLIDS

CICHLASOMA CITRINELLUM
Midas cichlid; lemon cichlid

Size: Up to 40cm(16in) long and 25cm(10in) deep.
Distribution: The southern part of Central America. In Nicaragua, it is found in the great lakes (Managua, Nicaragua and Jiloa) and also along the Atlantic coast of Costa Rica and south into northern Panama.

Not surprisingly, this fish takes its common name from its highly attractive golden yellow colour. The head is very steep and robust, with thick solid lips. Very young fish are silver and often show dark bars. As they mature, the bright yellow colour develops over the entire body, although some individuals may display random black and white blotches. Sexing this species is not too difficult; females may have pointed fins, but the male's fins are much longer, with very long ray extensions to the soft dorsal and anal fins.

One characteristic that this species has become renowned for is its large, fleshy head bulge, or 'nuchal hump'. The exact function of this growth is unknown. It develops with age, more so in males, and seems to be some form of dominance display. Females also develop the hump to

some extent, especially during spawning, but with females it regresses slightly once spawning is over. Many of the more recent aquarium introductions from Central America also develop this hump, often to an even greater degree, such as *C. synspilum*.

The midas cichlid has two close relations: the red devil (*Cichlasoma labiatum*) and the arrow cichlid (*C. zaliosum*). The red devil is virtually identical in shape, size and behaviour to *C. citrinellum*, but its colour is red rather than yellow, and its lips are thicker. It may be that many of the fishes in the hobby today are hybrids between *C. citrinellum* and *C. labiatum*. *C. zaliosum* is a dark-barred fish, rarely seen in the hobby. Both these species require the same care as the midas cichlid.

As a general rule, Central American cichlids are more aggressive than their South American counterparts and *C. citrinellum* is no exception. With some degree of luck, it can be educated to accept non-cichlid tankmates or cichlids of a different species, but this fish will very rarely accept inmates of its own kind. It seems to have no distaste for bright lighting in the aquarium, although you will have to consider the needs of all the occupants in this regard. Provide plenty of caves as protection for other fish.

In the wild, large caves formed by rocks and fallen trees form the territory for this fish. Here, it hides in wait for the small fishes – often young midas cichlids – that form part of its diet. When not hunting fish, this species will eat snails, molluscs and crustaceans, and occasionally removes the odd scale from other fishes as a snack. In the aquarium, the midas cichlid fortunately learns to accept other foods, including worms, beef heart and food pellets.

Midas cichlids breed quite readily. The female selects a site and she (or occasionally the pair) digs a huge hole close by. This will be used as a nursery to accommodate the non-swimming wriggling fry (called zygotes at this stage) during their first few days of life. About 800 eggs are laid on a flat rock and guarded by both parents. If there are any other fish in the aquarium at this time, they should be removed for their own safety. Many breeding attempts are abandoned prematurely as a result of this fish's highly aggressive behaviour, which may even lead to the death of the female. Observe breeding midas cichlids carefully;

Above: *In the male midas cichlid, a well-developed nuchal hump is a common feature.*

Below: Cichlasoma festae, *a close relative of* C. citrinellum *and often confused with it.*

there is little warning of impending friction and battles are usually short and sweet.

If several breeding attempts fail, it is worth trying the 'incomplete divider' breeding method. Place a piece of glass in the aquarium to separate the male and female. Put a piece of slate underneath the glass as a spawning site and raise the glass one centimetre above the slate (taking care that neither fish can swim through the gap). With luck, the female will spawn on her side of the slate and the male will fertilize his side. Enough sperm will migrate under the glass to fertilize a good proportion of the eggs and, as so many eggs are laid, the losses are affordable. If a pair are to be spawned without resorting to this method, make sure that their tank measures at least 120cm(48in) long for safety purposes.

CICHLASOMA DOVII
Wolf cichlid

Size: Males up to 75cm(30in), females no more than 40cm(16in).
Distribution: Widespread in Central America, from southern Honduras in the north as far south as Costa Rica.

The wolf cichlid, as its common name suggests, is one of the major predators of the piscine world. Its scientific name, 'dovii', on the other hand, seems misleading, suggesting a peaceful dove. In fact, it derives from Captain John Dow, a collector of fishes in the middle of the nineteenth century (though why a 'v' has been substituted for the 'w' in the scientific name is unclear). The body of the wolf cichlid is pure muscle, which enables this very slender, lean fish to move extremely quickly and with great power. The very thick muscular caudal peduncle and the large round tail are ideal for driving such a large fish through water at speed. The eyes are set well back on the head and face forward, typical of a top predator. At least two very prominent incisor teeth are visible, protruding upwards from the lower jaw.

As with many *Nandopsis* species (Central American predators), of which this is one, the adults are quite easy to sex. (This reference to *Nandopsis* may appear confusing; it is simply one of the 'sections' that has been created within the species *Cichlasoma*.) Juvenile specimens are fairly uninteresting silver fishes, with a broken horizontal stripe running along the flanks, but as they mature, males develop longer, more pointed fins, with a number of small spots. There are also several small spots on the head. Females, on the other hand, rarely show any spots at all and their base colour matures to a mustard yellow. As this fish has a large natural range, its colours often vary. Depending on origin, males may occasionally have a purple base colour.

Males grow far larger than females, with a much more powerful head. *Cichlasoma dovii* is one of the largest Central American cichlids; in fact it is one of the largest of all the cichlid species. This fish is a pure predator; in its natural habitat, it is rarely interested in eating anything other than fish. Furthermore, the adult fish does not hide from its prey, but roams about openly in extremely clear and very clean waters. Younger specimens cannot afford to display such bold behaviour, preferring to hide among the rocks to avoid becoming a meal for their older relatives.

Despite its predatory behaviour, the wolf cichlid is very timid in the aquarium. Provide plenty of caves and low lighting levels. Feeding can be a problem with newly acquired fishes. They often refuse anything other than live fish, but eventually they can be persuaded to accept more readily available food. A 150cm(60in) tank is the minimum requirement for a large adult fish. As it comes from very clean waters, it is highly intolerant of any dissolved metabolic wastes, so carry out large water changes on a regular basis. Take care when selecting tankmates; any fish much smaller than the wolf could easily be heading down the same path as Little Red Riding Hood!

Wolf cichlids rarely breed in captivity, but there are reports of spawnings when the fish reach about 13cm(5in). They prefer to spawn on a piece of rock with a slight incline and some cover, but will use any rock if there is no other choice. They may lay as many as 1,500 eggs, so it will be necessary to cull many of the fry.

Below: The predatory wolf cichlid is rarely aggressive towards fishes that it cannot easily eat and that it does not see as a threat in the tank.

CICHLASOMA MANAGUENSE
Jaguar; Managua jaguar

Size: 30cm(12in) – rarely to 50cm(20in).
Distribution: Honduras, Nicaragua (The Great Lakes) and Costa Rica.

Nearly all cichlids go through a colour change as they mature, and this most attractive fish is no exception. Young jaguars are a drab silver, with a broken horizontal line of black spots running along the torpedo-shaped body. As it approaches adulthood, its drabness is even greater, until suddenly, with the imminent onset of sexual maturity, things start to change. Drab blotches become darker and darker, eventually turning black. The common name 'jaguar cichlid' comes from this profusion of black spots (like the jaguar cat), which cover the whole of the male fish's body. In the female, they are less extensive. The base colour intensifies and, depending on the cichlid's origins, may be either bright golden yellow or copper. All the fins, apart from the pectorals, exhibit the same beautiful black patterning.

C. *managuense* is one of the top cichlid predators and can travel at great speed. One endearing feature is its lower lip, which often reveals two to four quite small, but prominent, incisor teeth. Although this fish is a predator, it is by no means aggressive for its size and while it may often take a dislike to cichlid species that are similar in colour and size to itself, such as C. *dovii*, it will tolerate most other dissimilar cichlids, as long as they remain subordinate. However, any fish that might possibly fit into the huge mouth of a jaguar cichlid should not be kept in the same aquarium.

Keeping this fish in good health is quite simple. A sufficiently large aquarium is essential; as a guide, it should measure at least five times the length of the fish. Despite its natural predatory behaviour, this fish is quite timid, perhaps because it is a popular food fish for Nicaraguans! Plenty of rockwork, along with caves and low lighting, will help the jaguar to settle down and feel at home. Although its natural food is live fish, the jaguar soon learns to take prepared food, such as prawns or raw fish along with pelleted foods.

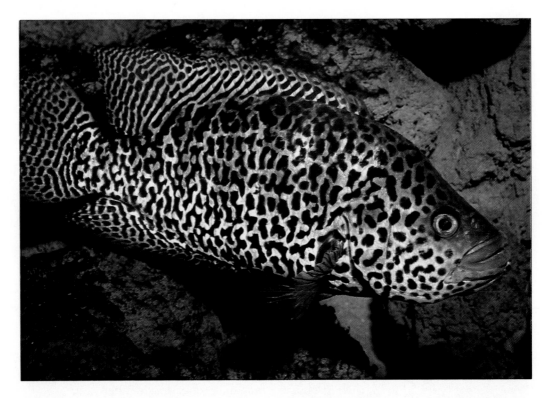

Sexing C. *managuense* is quite easy, once it has attained a total length of 13cm(5in) or more. At this stage, males become very aggressive towards tankmates and their colours intensify. The long, black, broken horizontal bar begins to disappear amid the many black spots that are now present. Females are far less colourful and, if well fed, develop a much plumper body and abdomen. Genital papillae are the best sexing guide. In well-fed fish, the male tube is only slightly visible, swept back and very narrow. In females, the papillae are broader and more perpendicular to the body.

Cichlasoma managuense spawns readily. In the wild, it is said to spawn in caves, but due to its large size, this is rarely possible in an aquarium. The pair usually select a flat rock and lay eggs and fertilize them alternately in typical cichlid fashion. About 2,000-3,000 eggs are laid and guarded by the female, while the male surveys the perimeter for predators. The eggs hatch after three days and the fry are free swimming five days later. At this point, the aquarist must cull the fry dramatically if any specimens are to grow at a proper rate and attain their full adult size.

Above: *This Managua jaguar is one of the most attractive large cichlids.*

The copper form is a particularly desirable fish for the aquarium.

CICHLASOMA SPECIES. CF. MOTAGUENSE
Yellow guapote

Size: Up to 25cm(10in).
Distribution: Mexico, southern Guatemala and El Salvador.

The taxonomic status of many cichlids remains uncertain and confusion frequently reigns. One case in point is the yellow guapote (pronounced gwa-poe-tay). For several years, this fish was known as *Cichlasoma motaguense* but it is now accepted not as a colour sport of *C. motaguense* but as a distinct species.

In most specimens, the yellow coloration is outstanding. Indeed, coloration is a very good guide to the sex of the fish, once they are mature. Young specimens are silvery olive, with a long unbroken line and often show several bars. As they mature, their beauty starts to shine through. Males have a base colour of bright canary yellow, overlaid with a purple and grey bloom that covers most of the dorsal area. The long horizontal line along the body of the juvenile breaks up and becomes eight or nine blotches, ending in a round spot at the tail. The male also develops black or brown blotches on the belly. In addition, the male is decorated with many fine spots in the dorsal, anal and caudal fins. The base colour of the female is more orange. She lacks the fine spots in the fins and has less black blotches in the belly. Both fish show a couple of black 'tear drop' markings underneath the eye.

Like the wolf cichlid, the yellow guapote also belongs to the *Nandopsis* section of American cichlids, all of which are predatory to some degree, but this fish is less aggressive and predatory than *C. dovii*. In the aquarium, it is relatively peaceful, ignoring most other tank occupants when it is spawning. These fish can be safely kept and spawned in an aquarium as small as 75cm(30in), but a 90cm(36in) tank would make a better home. Set up some type of cave system in the aquarium; in moments of shyness, this fish likes to beat a hasty retreat to some secluded spot.

Feeding the yellow guapote is relatively easy; it snatches greedily at live food, especially earthworms, and will accept beef heart, raw fish, prawns and frozen blood-worm. It also has a taste for vegetable matter, so offer green food occasionally.

These cichlids will breed without much difficulty and make excellent parents. Having selected a smooth surface, such as a piece of slate or a flat area on a piece of bogwood, the pair clean the site fastidiously for several days, while their spawning tubes begin to lower. Eventually, the female starts to attach her eggs to the surface in small runs of 20 or 30 and the male intervenes to fertilize the eggs as each row or two is laid. When the 800 or so eggs have been produced, the female mounts guard above them, while the male protects the outskirts of the spawning territory from potential predators. If there are other fish in the aquarium, things may now start to get violent, with the male chasing them away. The eggs hatch after three days and the fry becoming free swimming after a further four days, when they will need feeding with dust-fine particles of flake food or newly hatched brineshrimps.

Below: *When it is not spawning, the attractive yellow guapote is rarely aggressive towards other fishes. Only the smallest species risk being eaten.*

CICHLASOMA NICARAGUENSE
Nicaragua cichlid; macaw cichlid

Size: Males up to 25cm(10in); females up to 18cm(7in).
Distribution: Nicaragua and Costa Rica.

Some Central American cichlids are relatively new to the hobby and, as in this case, their common names are not always widely recognized. However, there is no mistaking this cichlid's stunning coloration, which has ensured its popularity among fishkeepers. The head is a beautiful slate grey, with a tinge of purple on the operculum. The rest of the body is bright orange, with all the scales outlined and very prominent. The fins are also orange, but the dorsal fin has a turquoise edge. All the fins are decorated with a profusion of small, dark orange-brown spots. The female is much smaller, with a bright turquoise head and even more intense tangerine body coloration. She lacks outlines to the scales and has no spots in her fins. As juveniles, both male and female have a long horizontal black line, but the male tends to lose this line with age and shows just a central spot. Occasionally, the line remains apparent.

Unfortunately, there is a tendency for some dealers to overcrowd their tanks and in less than ideal conditions the true colours

Above: In Cichlasoma nicaraguense *the female is often more colourful than the male, which is rare in nature.*

Below: Male specimens of C. nicaraguense *can be identified by the fine spots on their longer, pointed unpaired fins.*

of *C. nicaraguense* may fail to develop. If you can bring yourself to accept a drab-looking fish, you may well pick up a bargain. A juvenile or 'depressed' adult is usually silver with a single horizontal line along the length of the body. Given a warm tank (26°C/79°F) and peaceful companions, it will soon alter beyond recognition.

C. nicaraguense has a very small underslung mouth and uses its clearly visible, tiny teeth to bite at rocks, removing algae and crustaceans for food. In its natural environment, it is often found in the same waters as the wolf cichlid (*C. dovii*), and there is a theory for this association. A third fish, *Neetroplus nematopus*, also lives in the same region and competes with *C. nicaraguense* for breeding caves. The Nicaragua cichlid is said to look after the fry of the wolf cichlid along with its own, so that when these grow, they prey on the *Neetroplus nematopus*, thus leaving more caves for *C. nicaraguense*. As the Nicaragua and wolf cichlid share this affiliation, they usually make ideal tankmates. Both are intolerant of poor water quality, so make frequent partial water changes.

The Nicaragua cichlid is quite easily spawned and unique in its method of breeding. The pair excavate a large pit inside a cave – preferably one with a very small entrance – and the female lays some 300 to 400 eggs, which the male fertilizes. These eggs are not adhesive, as in all other known neotropical cichlids. Instead, they are guarded by the parents but, again, unlike other cichlids, the adults do very little fanning or mouthing of the eggs, which are mostly left to 'bobble' about until they hatch some three days later.

CICHLASOMA ROBERTSONI
Blue sifter

Size: Males about 23cm(9in); females up to 18cm(7in) maximum.
Distribution: Southern Mexico, Guatemala and Belize.

The blue sifter is one of the new – and very welcome – arrivals in the aquarium world and, as it becomes more available, its popularity is sure to grow. It takes its common name from its coloration and its habit of taking up mouthfuls of substrate, sifting it for food and then spitting it out. It belongs to the *Amphilophus* section of *Cichlasoma*, a group containing predators, opportunistic feeders and specialist feeders to some degree.

The head of this fish is very steep, the body short and squat. The dorsal and anal fins are pointed, the caudal fin round. The base colour of the body is light olive to lime

Below: C. robertsoni *behaves more like a* Geophagus *species; its* *constant gravel-sifting means that it requires a non-coarse substrate.*

green and, running vertically, are about 10 or 11 narrow black bars, one of which fades into the eye. There is a central black spot on the flanks and the whole body, particularly the lower half and including the gill cover, is covered in a profusion of small, light blue spots. This is one of the most attractive fish to make its appearance for a long time, but sexing it is almost impossible. As a guide, males have a larger, more steeply sloping head and very slightly longer fins. Females are less robust and not so domineering.

In the wild, the blue sifter is found in slow-moving rivers and lagoons, often in the same haunts as the large predator *Petenia splendida*, the bay snook. In the aquarium, it spends most of its time searching the substrate for food with its small underslung mouth. It is important to supply food that falls quickly to the bottom of the tank, otherwise the surface-feeders will capture the lion's share. Because *C. robertsoni* constantly sifts the substrate, it is safer to provide fairly fine substrate material, since large particles easily become stuck in the fish's mouth, causing it to choke or suffocate.

It is quite a timid fish, so keep the lighting levels reasonably low. The blue sifter appreciates the company of other non-aggressive fish that match its temperament, and this will help to reduce its shyness. Flowerpot caves provide ideal cover.

As the blue sifter is quite new to the hobby, it has not been bred very often. The easiest way to obtain a pair is to place five or six fishes in an aquarium and let them pair off naturally. Once a pair bond is formed, both male and female excavate a large pit, usually in an open space where the pair can get a good view in all directions and survey potential predators. The female then proceeds to lay her eggs on the substrate at the base of the pit in runs of 10 to 20, the male fertilizing them in between each run. Up to 1,000 eggs may be laid, although half this number is more common. Both male and female guard and fan the eggs, but in most cases the female assumes the major responsibility for this chore. The fry hatch in 72 hours and become free swimming after a further four days. They are guarded by their parents against all other tank occupants, regardless of size.

CICHLASOMA SYNSPILUM
Quetzal

Size: Males up to 40cm(16in); females about 23cm(9in).
Distribution: Northern Central America, in particular Mexico, Guatemala and Belize.

Cichlasoma synspilum is one of the most popular large cichlids. It takes its common name from a large and colourful Guatemalan bird, which is very appropriate, as this is an extremely colourful fish when adult. The quetzal is one of 20 or so that form the *Theraps* section of *Cichlasoma*. These fish are all opportunistic feeders, some almost scavengers. The majority are indistinguishable when young and several are quite difficult to distinguish even when adult. Until they attain 7.5cm(3in) in total length, nearly all are silver with a black arc running from the tail to the operculum.

As the quetzal grows, this arc breaks up into several blotches that gradually fade until only one or two are left at the tail, and even these may become quite faint. The body is relatively deep and the mouth points very slightly down, the top lip protruding a little above the lower. At about 10cm(4in), the quetzal develops subtle colours that gradually intensify with age. The head begins to turn flamingo pink, often darker, and the body becomes golden orange, with many reflective shades of blue, green and turquoise at the tail and in the fins. Many small, dark spots develop in the dorsal and anal fins, particularly in the male. This is one of the larger cichlids; males have no trouble reaching 30cm(12in) in total length if fed well on a varied diet and given regular water changes.

The quetzal is difficult to sex, as there are no apparent morphological differences. If several males are kept together, the dominant one may develop a large fatty lump on the top of its head. This can expand and contract to some degree, particularly during spawning. Unfortunately, this is no guarantee of masculinity, as females can also develop these so-called nuchal humps. (The word 'nuchal' refers to the nape of the neck.)

In its natural habitat, the quetzal frequents slow-moving rivers and

backwaters, even dark and murky streams. Here, it spends most of its time picking through the vegetation and pecking over the muddy bottom. In captivity, these fish are opportunistic feeders, readily accepting most foods, including earthworms, pellets, beef heart and prawns. However, it is very important to offer vegetable matter; the quetzal is particularly fond of sweet corn and garden peas with the skins removed.

When young, the quetzal is extremely timid and will dash for cover at the slightest disturbance. As it grows, it gains in confidence. Young individuals always fare

Left: *The quetzal is yet another cichlid that develops a pronounced nuchal hump. This is more prominent with age and when spawning.*

Below: *Provide a large aquarium for breeding purposes. The quetzal often prefers to hide its newly hatched fry under a large rocky crevice.*

better in the company of other quetzals or appropriate juvenile cichlids.

The adults usually spawn on a large flat surface, such as a rock, but the pair may excavate down to the undergravel filter plates if the opportunity is there. The female lays in the region of 1,500 to 2,000 eggs in a comparatively massive spread, approximately 15cm(6in) square. About 10 percent of the eggs are not adhesive and these are regarded as disposable by the parents, and eaten.

The fry hatch after three days and are then placed in some concealed crevice or under a rock by their parents. After a further five days, they become free swimming and rise up in a huge cloud to surround their parents. At this stage, they need to be well fed, otherwise they will supplement their diet by pecking at the parents' mucus and fins. If 1,500 fry are allowed to do this unchecked, it will prove detrimental to the health of the parents. Fine flake food and newly hatched brineshrimp are ideal initial foods.

CICHLASOMA TRIMACULATUM
Tri-mac; three-spot cichlid

Size: Males up to 38cm(15in); females up to 25cm(10in).
Distribution: The Pacific coast of Central America, from Mexico in the north as far south as El Salvador.

This is undoubtedly one of the largest and most stunning cichlids in the aquarium world. The common name 'tri-mac' derives from the Latin *trimaculatum*, meaning 'three spots'. In the wild, *C. trimaculatum* is an adaptable fish and because of its ability to live in brackish lagoons it has managed to migrate along the coastline via the sea. Its natural habitats are slow-moving rivers and backwaters. Here it hides among dense reed-beds, ready to pounce on potential

Below: The tri-mac will battle with its own species for dominance of the whole aquarium. The often huge size difference between male and female make this a difficult fish to spawn successfully.

prey, such as crustaceans and small fish, including younger tri-macs. This fish belongs to the *Amphilophus* section of cichlids and is partly predatory, partly opportunistic in its feeding habits.

This very deep solid fish probably weighs more than any other cichlid of comparable length. Like most cichlids, the young specimens do not greatly resemble adults. Until it reaches 7.5cm(3in), the tri-mac is an uninteresting silver fish with three black spots along its body, one behind the eye, one in the centre of the flank and one at the tail. There may be one of two other insignificant spots in between. The only outstanding characteristics at this age are the deep ruby red eyes and a slight pinkness to the throat. However, as the fish grows, the body takes on a lovely yellow-green hue, each of the spots becomes encircled with bright metallic blue and the eyes grow larger and more intense in colour. The pink throat eventually reddens until it is extremely dark, often claret coloured.

The tri-mac is difficult to sex when young, but the differences become clearer with age. Females remain much smaller and less brightly coloured, while males develop longer fins decorated with small spots. Males also develop quite a large fatty growth on top of the head.

Tri-macs are not the easiest cichlids to breed. Although young juveniles tolerate each other, adults rarely do, and only when you have established a compatible pair can you hope to keep two fishes together in one tank. There are other complications; although these fish are said to be open breeders in the wild, in the aquarium they often spawn in a cave. The female makes this choice and if she picks a cave that is too small for the male, fighting may occur. Often, there is little advance warning of impending friction between a pair, and if the male is considerably larger than the female any battle is likely to end with the death of the female.

Successful spawnings start with the pair cleaning a rock and digging a large pit adjacent to it. The female lays about 800 or more eggs and these are alternately fertilized by the male in rows of 20 or so, eventually forming a large round patch. At this stage, the female's vertical bar markings (which are rarely visible) become very prominent and almost fuse together to produce a virtually black fish, the only other colour being a slight reddening to the throat, some slight olive body coloration and an intense red eye. She then guards and fans the eggs, racing towards any intruder at surprising speed. It only takes one assault by such an intimidating fish to force all its tankmates to retire to a corner.

The eggs hatch in three days and the fry are free swimming and feeding after another four or five days. As they develop, they become increasingly nasty towards each other, especially after reaching about 5cm(2in) long, and thus the whole cycle starts again. While this fish can quite happily be kept on its own in a 90cm(36in) aquarium, never attempt to breed it in a tank measuring less than 120cm(48in).

CICHLASOMA UMBRIFERUM
The umbee

Size: Males up to 50cm(20in); females up to 25cm(10in).
Distribution: Eastern Panama and northern Colombia.

The finest Central American cichlid has been saved till last – the umbee, *Cichlasoma umbriferum*. If ever an animal was all muscle, mouth and stomach, then this is it. Its role in the aquarium is to strive for outright dominance. It is not entirely accurate to describe this fish as Central American, as the bulk of its range is in South America, but its behaviour is pure Central American. When young, it lives in peace with all other fish except for another umbee. As this beast grows, however, it works its way up the pecking order of the aquarium, submitting each tankmate in turn to a barrage of physical onslaughts until the victim's scales are removed and its fins torn. The vigilant fishkeeper must be quick to remove any damaged fish, otherwise they will die. The umbee is easily antagonized and not afraid to take on fish much larger than itself, even tankmates that have been established in the aquarium for some time. Eventually, you are left with the umbee on

its own or, possibly, in the company of a persistent catfish, such as a *Hypostomus* sp. Usually, only the aquarium glass and rocks can sustain such punishment. Despite all this, however, the umbee is still quite a timid fish when young and appreciates low lighting levels. As it grows, it becomes completely outgoing and will often try to penetrate the front glass to bite any passers-by.

This highly desirable cichlid often arrives as part of a consignment of other South American fishes, such as pike cichlids (*Crenicichla*) or acaras (*Aequidens*), usually measuring about 7.5cm(3in) long. At this age, it is a very uninteresting looking fish, reasonably slender, often emaciated. It is silvery gold in colour, with a small black spot on the side. As it matures, it develops a deep orange back and brass-coloured belly, overlaid with a profusion of blue speckles, which are particularly intense on the operculum. The dorsal and anal fins develop very long ray extensions, two or three of which may trail past the end of the tail. The squat females are far less spectacular, attaining only half the size of the male. They do not develop any long ray extensions and their coloration is less bright, lacking many of the male's metallic blue spots.

The scientific name *umbriferum* means 'shadow' or 'shady', a reference to the rather unusual mottled appearance that this fish can display when frightened or stalking its prey. Its natural habitats are rivers and pools where the light is often obscured by the trees and vegetation above. It lurks among reed-beds and fallen trees or caves, waiting for its prey.

The young umbee is quite demanding where feeding is concerned. It generally accepts earthworms, raw fish and beef heart, but every cichlid is an individual and one specimen may take a dislike to any of these foods. Live fish is certainly the best and most natural food, but once the umbee has been fed live fish it will be reluctant to change its diet. By feeding live fish, you could be making a rod for your own back, given their limited supply. With good feeding and careful maintenance, however, *C. umbriferum* can become a really impressive specimen, growing even larger than the average sizes quoted.

As this is such a large and aggressive fish, breeding is seldom accomplished. Nevertheless, if you wish to keep a large cichlid on its own in a 'pet' situation, there is no more spectacular showpiece.

AFRICAN CICHLIDS

CYPHOTILAPIA FRONTOSA
Frontosa

Size: Males up to 30cm(12in); females somewhat smaller.
Distribution: Lake Tanganyika

Many cichlids, including a number of Central American species, develop a large fatty growth on the top of the head, known as a nuchal hump. *Cyphotilapia frontosa* takes its name from this characteristic, which is more pronounced and outstanding in this species than in almost any other. The precise reason for its development is uncertain; most theories attribute it to some form of masculine status symbol, as the more dominant males develop the greater nuchal humps, but females may also develop them to a lesser extent.

The frontosa is quite a peaceful fish, probably less aggressive than any of the cichlid species discussed so far. If it is to feel happy in its environment, its tankmates should be of a similar disposition.

Most newcomers to the cichlid hobby cannot fail to be enchanted by the small juveniles for sale in aquarium shops. At 5cm(2in), the fish are snow white, with five or six jet black or dark grey bars. All the fins are a beautiful light blue, as is the snout and the trailing edge of the operculum. The small mouth is very low on the head and the lips are quite thick.

As this fish grows, it changes quite considerably. The black bars thicken until they almost obscure the white base colour. The large nuchal hump begins to develop, growing even larger with age, and the fins lengthen and develop long ray extensions. Some individuals may show an additional vertical bar or slightly different colouring in the fins. These are not a guide to sexual status, but geographical variants.

One of the main characteristics of the frontosa's natural habitat is the hardness and cleanliness of the water. To maintain this fish successfully, you must emulate these conditions. Water hardness needs to be 20°dH or more and the nitrite level

Below: *As a juvenile, the frontosa's bars are very vivid, but with age these markings become somewhat washed out and merged together.*

should be zero. Increase hardness by adding cockleshell particles to the substrate, or a proprietary brand of hardening substrate, and incorporating calciferous stone as decor. The filtration system must incorporate a very good biological system and, if this is via an undergravel filter, then a gravel tidy is an asset.

Feeding is relatively simple. *C. frontosa* is a bottom dweller, and requires some form of non-floating food. As well as flaked food, it enjoys small pieces of fish, prawn and frozen bloodworm.

The frontosa is a maternal mouthbrooder and, given the correct water quality and frequent water changes, is quite likely to spawn, although often there is little advance warning of such behaviour. When a pair decide to spawn, the male may start chasing all other tankmates away from the chosen spawning site. Then the female lays her non-adhesive eggs in ones or twos, moving in a tight circle with the male. He deposits his sperm and the female immediately picks up the eggs in her mouth. This process continues until all the eggs are laid. Depending on the condition and size of the female, the number of eggs can range from two or three to 20, 30 or quite a few more.

After five or six weeks, depending on the water temperature, the fry are released from the female's mouth, but for a further week or so they may be taken back in if the female fears they are in danger. It is a good idea to provide plenty of rockwork for the fry to hide in during their first few months.

HAPLOCHROMIS ROSTRATUS
Beaked hap

Size: Males up to 25cm(10in); females up to 20cm(8in).
Distribution: Lake Malawi.

The beaked hap takes its scientific name from its beaklike snout, *rostratus* being Latin for 'beak'. It is found along many of the shores of Lake Malawi where the substrate is composed of fine sand. Here, it sifts through the substrate searching for small crustaceans and insects, often in the company of another cichlid, *Cyrtocara moorii*, the dolphin cichlid, also a bottom feeder.

The beaked hap is not difficult to feed and will accept most foods, including flaked foods, frozen bloodworm, prawns and raw fish. To reflect its natural diet, you can also offer woodlice and similar insects.

As small juveniles, both male and female look quite similar. The top of the fish is a light brown to dark grey, the flanks silver and very shiny. Along the flanks are five dark vertical blotches and there is also a small spot on the operculum and the caudal peduncle. At about 10-13cm(4-5in), the beaked hap starts to mature and the male develops his masculine coloration. The drab silver is gradually replaced, until the body is

a stunning blue overall, tinged with green in places. All the fins, including the pectorals, are the same blue coloration, and the tail has some small pale spots. Females remain a drab silver, similar to juveniles.

As with all Rift Valley Lake cichlids, *H. rostratus* requires very clean water conditions. Frequent partial water changes, and a good undergravel filter used in conjunction with an external mechanical filter are essential. The water should be hard and alkaline, with a pH level of 7.8-8.5 and a hardness of 17-20°dH.

It is not a good idea to keep these fish (or any other *Haplochromis* species for that matter) in pairs; they are highly aggressive and the stronger cichlid will often bully the weaker one. By keeping a number of fish together, aggression is diluted and no single fish takes the brunt of any violent behaviour. Provide plenty of rockwork caves so that subordinate fish can hide from their belligerent elders. Females are often subjected to a great deal of bullying from males wishing to spawn.

H. rostratus is a typical mouthbrooder. A courtship display, accompanied by an enormous increase in aggression in the male, precedes the spawning. The male flutters his fins in order to attract the female and with his nose down and tail quivering, he hovers over a chosen site. Eventually, the female lays one or two large eggs on the substrate and, once they have been fertilized by the male, she collects them into her mouth. Sometimes, she takes the sperm into her mouth and fertilization takes place there. The eggs are then rotated and 'chewed over' in her mouth for some four or five weeks until, eventually, exact miniature replicas of the adult female are released.

HEMICHROMIS ELONGATUS
Five-spot cichlid

Size: Up to 18cm(7in).
Distribution: The rivers of West and Central Africa, particularly in Guinea, Liberia, Nigeria and Zaire.

There are many *Hemichromis* species, the most common being the popular (and slightly varying) jewel cichlids. Easily overlooked as a drab juvenile, *H. elongatus* develops its stunning coloration as it grows. At only 2.5cm(1in) long, the five large black spots are already visible along the flanks, stretching almost from the top of the body to the bottom in certain moods. Another black line runs diagonally through the eye. Gradually, the edge of the dorsal and anal fin begin to show a light blue coloration. The scales are all quite prominent and many of the central rows have a deep red hue. The deep red markings on the trailing edge of the operculum are a useful aid in distinguishing this fish from its close cousin *Hemichromis fasciatus*, which is a similar colour when young but attains an adult length of 43cm(17in). As the five-spot cichlid matures, its body turns from silver to yellow, making it an extremely attractive fish. There are no clear sexual differences, but, with age, males may show a more solid head and may sometimes develop a slight nuchal hump.

Left: *In* Haplochromis rostratus, *the females are smaller and far less showy than the colourful male fishes.*

Below: *Maintain water quality at the highest standards to ensure that males achieve a good size and coloration.*

Above: Hemichromis
elongatus *is literally
a pocket battleship in*
*every sense of the word.
It is probably the most
powerful of the cichlids.*

It is not size that makes the five-spot cichlid so interesting, rather its sheer power and aggression. In its wild state, the five-spot cichlid is an out and out predator, hiding among rocks and vegetation in order to pounce on any unsuspecting young fish. It is a pocket battleship in every sense of the word, and definitely takes no prisoners. Should another fish happen to take a small nip out of its fins, the five-spot retaliates tenfold, never appreciating the meaning of a measured response. For this reason, always house it with fish twice its own size.

Because it is so aggressive, do not even consider keeping *H. elongatus* in an aquarium with other fishes unless the tank is over 90cm(36in) long. Even if you provide plenty of caves for the other fish to hide in, remember that the five-spot will also hide in these caves, waiting for its prey. Lighting levels are unimportant, but water quality should be high. The five-spot thrives in hard water with a moderate pH. Feeding is quite simple; it greedily accepts food pellets, beef heart, prawns and raw fish.

Spawning may be fraught with difficulty, and the only way to obtain a pair is to place several individuals together in an aquarium and wait for a natural pairing. If a pairing does occur, remove the other cichlids. The pair will select a rock and, after a great deal of cleaning, the female proceeds to lay her eggs in a series of short strings. The male breaks in to fertilize them and eventually there will be some 500 or so in a large flat mass. The pair excavate a huge crater to receive the young. Rearing is the same as for other bi-parental substrate-spawners, such as *Cichlasoma citrinellum* and *C. trimaculatum* (see pages 128 and 138).

TILAPIA BUTTIKOFERI
Tilapia

Size: Up to 40cm(16in) in captivity, often much smaller in their natural habitat.
Distribution: West Africa, in Guinea and Liberia.

Tilapia buttikoferi is another West African cichlid and one of the largest of all the African cichlid species. Although these prolific fish are endemic to Africa, they have been introduced to the Americas in order to provide food for the underdeveloped countries. Unfortunately, they often damage the native fish populations, some of which may become extinct. Furthermore, much of the human population find the fish less appetizing than their usual catch.

Although it does not have stunning coloration, *T. buttikoferi* has a very interesting colour pattern, and this makes it a welcome addition to any large aquarium housing very robust species. The body is very deep – indeed, half as deep as it is long. The base colour is light beige, overlaid with eight distinct vertical dark grey bars. All the unpaired fins are dark grey or almost black, whereas the ventral fins are black with a white leading edge. The colours of small juvenile fish are particularly vivid and distinct but, sadly, as they grow, the colours fade somewhat and become rather 'washed out'. Unfortunately, there is no way of distinguishing males from females, either by colour, build or fin development.

This is probably one of the most belligerent African cichlids. In its natural state it holds a large territory, and if you wish to house it in an aquarium with other fish, you must provide a suitably spacious tank, i.e. at least 135x45x45cm(54x18x18in). Unlike the Rift Valley Lake species, *Tilapia buttikoferi* thrives in most waters and does

not require the same hard, alkaline conditions. It is not a timid cichlid, so bright lighting is not a problem either.

In the wild, it spends its time among rocks, pecking over the bottom in search of food, particularly molluscs and crustaceans. In the aquarium, it is a less specialized feeder, greedily accepting worms, beef heart, raw fish, pellets and peas.

Tilapia buttikoferi is an open-breeding substrate-spawner. Once a pair bond is formed, both fish excavate a large pit with the intention of spawning on the solid base below. Spawning takes place with the pair alternating egg laying and fertilization. In the wild, *Tilapia* fry are preyed upon relentlessly and consequently spawns are enormous – in *T. buttikoferi's* case often well over 1,500 eggs. Unfortunately, this fish is highly aggressive at spawning time and pairs often fight in the confines of an aquarium. It may be necessary to breed these cichlids using the divided tank method, as described on page 130.

Below: Tilapia buttikoferi *is a large and popular show fish.*

Wild specimens often show more pronounced coloration and pattern.

SLEEPER GOBIES

The sleeper gobies belong to the family Eleotridae. They have separate ventral fins, whereas in the true gobies, of the family Gobiidae, these fins are united into a cup-shaped sucker. The body is elongate and cylindrical at the front, with two distinct dorsal fins. The first has shorter, flexible spines and the second shows soft rays, sometimes preceded by a single spine. The caudal fin is rounded and the anal fin is about as long as the second dorsal. The lateral line is usually absent. Larger species lose much of their colouring with age.

Most sleeper gobies are found in brackish to fresh waters throughout the world, although some species live only in fresh water. Some are predatory bottom-dwelling fishes that make rapid darting movements in search of fishes and invertebrates; others feed on plankton. They seldom swim in mid water, and then only clumsily. If you add marine salt to an aquarium housing species from brackish waters take care to choose suitable plants and companions.

Spawning methods vary. The genera *Dormitator* and *Mogurnda* spawn in a similar way to cichlids, depositing eggs on stones and wood. *Eleotris* spawns among fine-leaved plants, with males undertaking limited brood care, fanning the eggs with their pectoral fins and keeping the newly hatched fry together. The young are free-swimming initially and assume the bottom-dwelling habits of the adults later on. They grow rapidly on a diet of freshly hatched brineshrimp and *Daphnia*.

OXYELEOTRIS MARMORATUS
Marbled sleeper goby

Size: Up to 50cm(20in).
Distribution: Thailand, Malayan Peninsula, Sumatra, Borneo and Indonesia.

The marbled sleeper goby is one of the largest gobies. It inhabits slow-moving bodies of fresh water, where it is a nocturnal hunter. During daylight hours, it hides away in burrows or hollow logs, where its marbled, grey-brown patterning provides perfect camouflage. Not surprisingly, in the aquarium it requires many hiding places among rocks, wood and

plants, and a soft substrate. The water should not be too hard – about 10-15°dH, with a neutral pH level and a temperature of 22-26°C(72-79°F). This fish tends to dig and stir up the soft substrate when hunting for food, so the filtration system needs to be able to cope with this. An external power filter, regularly cleaned and used as a mechanical filter to remove most of the debris, combined with a biological, undertank filter system would be ideal.

The marbled sleeper goby is an exceedingly greedy fish, consuming its own weight in food every day. It accepts virtually any meaty food, from earthworms and insect larvae to pieces of fish and meat, but it prefers live food.

It is possible to distinguish between the sexes: males are more highly coloured, have a higher second dorsal fin, a longer anal fin and conical genital papillae; females are more uniformly coloured, with cyclindrical genital papillae.

Below left: *This river in Borneo bordered by a dense canopy of trees provides ideal living conditions for the marbled sleeper goby.*

Below: *Dawn and dusk are the best times to observe* Oxyeleotris marmoratus *and these are therefore good times at which to offer food.*

ANABANTIDS

There are four families of anabantids: Anabantidae, the climbing perches; Belontiidae, the gouramies and fighting fishes; Helostomatidae, with a single species, *Helostoma temmincki* – the kissing gourami; and Osphronemidae, again with a single species, *Osphronemus goramy* – the giant gourami. Most are small fishes, less than 20cm(8in) long, and the genera *Helostoma* and *Trichogaster* are considered to be community fishes. They are widespread, with representatives in Africa, India and Southeast Asia (including the Philippines).

All these fishes possess an accessory breathing organ that enables them to live in poorly oxygenated waters. In some genera, such as *Anabas*, the fish leave the water and climb onto roots and twigs.

Breeding strategies vary. In some species, males build bubblenests and guard these until the fry are free-swimming; in others, the eggs are brooded in the mouth; while other species produce floating eggs and the parents take no interest in them at all.

OSPHRONEMUS GORAMY
Giant gourami

Size: Up to 60cm(24in).
Distribution: China, eastern India, Malaysia and Java.

The giant gourami and *H. temmincki* are the only anabantids that could be classed as large. *O. goramy* is available as 5cm(2in) youngsters, and at this size they are attractively patterned with dark and light vertical bands. Given the right conditions, they grow rapidly, soon reaching 10cm(4in), but then the coloration changes and becomes a uniform grey-brown. Young fish

Below: This river in Malaysia provides a habitat for the giant gourami, a species that will flourish even in water low in oxygen.

Left: Adult specimens of O. goramy become very tame and will take a variety of foods from their keeper's hand.

Above: Young giant gouramis grow rapidly and will eat anything. Their attractive colour fades as they mature.

tend to fight one another, but individual specimens make ideal companions for other large fishes, and as the giant gourami matures, it loses some of its earlier pugnacious tendencies.

The giant gourami is omnivorous, eating anything from pelleted foods to plant material and smaller tankmates, but vegetable matter is essential to maintain it in top condition. These fish seem particularly fond of ripe banana, lettuce and peas. In Thailand, their rapid growth rate and willingness to consume almost anything has

resulted in the giant gourami being raised in ponds as a food fish, the flesh being regarded as a delicacy.

Breeding these fish in the aquarium is possible, as they mature at about six months. At this stage, the male is distinguishable by his pointed dorsal and anal fins and, during the spawning season, his thickened lips. Both parents help to build a 15cm(6in) diameter nest, in shallow water, about 30cm(12in) from the substrate and 20cm(8in) below the surface. (Clearly they are particular about the depth of water in which they breed.) The nest consists largely of plant material, with relatively few of the mucus-coated bubbles normally associated with anabantids. The floating eggs, about 2.5mm(0.1in) in diameter, can take up to a month to hatch, and the fry are then guarded by the male until, at about two weeks old, they leave the nest.

SNAKEHEADS

Snakeheads are found in Africa and Southeast Asia. They are elongate, with small ventral fins. In one species, *Channa asiatica*, these fins are absent. The dorsal and anal fins are long-based and composed of soft rays. Snakeheads have an accessory breathing organ that enables them to travel overland to new watercourses in periods of drought, and they can also survive in muddy, oxygen-deficient waters.

These stealthy predators often approach their prey from the front, coil their body into an 'S'-shape and then strike, much like a snake striking a rat. Although they appreciate live food in their diet, they can be raised without any problems on a variety of meaty foods, such as prawns (complete with shells for larger specimens), pieces of fish, meat, insect larvae and worms, etc. They will also take food from the hand.

Snakeheads spend a great deal of time lurking among vegetation and require a well-planted aquarium. They adapt to most water conditions, as long as extremes of hardness and pH are avoided. A biological filtration system, combined with an external filter, is essential to cope with the waste produced by these heavy feeders.

Snakeheads jump, so be sure to provide a tight-fitting lid on the aquarium. Should the fish escape, you may find it in a somewhat desiccated condition on the floor, but before giving up hope completely, replace it in the aquarium. With the aid of their accessory breathing apparatus, these tenacious fish can survive for some time if the atmosphere is not too dry.

Some species have been bred in captivity. The large eggs contain droplets of oil that cause them to rise to the surface. They develop quickly, the young hatching in two to three days at a temperature of 26-28°C (79-82°F). They remain at the surface, belly-up until the yolk sac is absorbed and only then, some six to eight days after hatching, are the fry able to leave the surface and swim normally. The eggs and fry are guarded by their parents.

Below: *A river in Thailand, the typical environment of* Channa *sp. Snakeheads thrive in muddy waters and can survive drying out.*

CHANNA MICROPELTES

Size: Up to 90cm(36in).
Distribution: India, Burma, Thailand, Malaysia and Indonesia.

This is one of the largest snakeheads. Small specimens are very attractive and frequently offered as aquarium fish. They grow rapidly. The background colour is silvery white and two black bars with a red bar inbetween run along the flanks of the fish. As the fish grows, this red band breaks up into a series of spots and blotches, the dorsal surface becomes brownish, but the belly remains white.

This very pugnacious fish has a reputation among anglers in Thailand for being a very good sporting fish that puts up a great fight once hooked. It demonstrates the same belligerence when guarding its nest and eggs, even attacking humans fearlessly if threatened.

When several specimens are kept together in an aquarium, bullying usually results and weaker fishes are prevented from reaching

Above: Given a variety of meaty foods, most of the snakeheads grow rapidly. This Channa striata *is no exception.*

Below: This Channa micropeltes, *the largest of the snakeheads, loses its beautiful juvenile colouring as it matures.*

food. Fatalities are not uncommon. *Channa micropeltes* is an active predator, consuming vast quantities of fish and killing far more than it can actually eat. It will attack other fishes in the aquarium, so be sure to choose suitably large companions for them.

SPINY EELS

Spiny eels are found in the fresh and brackish waters of tropical Africa, in India through Burma, Thailand and into Malaysia and China. Despite their appearance, they have no relationship to the true eels. The head is elongated and the snout is long, fleshy and movable. The dorsal fin consists of a row of individual spines that can be raised and lowered at will, and these give the fish their common name. They lack ventral fins.

Typically crepuscular (i.e. active at dawn and dusk), they spend much of the day hidden among plants or buried in the substrate, only venturing out to forage for small worms and insect larvae, which they find using the highly mobile snout. Once located, the food is sucked into the mouth with a jerking head motion.

One of the spiny eels, *Mastacemblus pancalus*, has been bred in captivity. Males pursue the females, nudging them in the region of the vent and the eggs are probably scattered over the substrate. There are no details of hatching times. The young fishes hide among plants and in the substrate.

MASTACEMBLUS ARMATUS
Tyre-track eel

Size: Up to 75cm(30in).
Distribution: Southern China, India, Sri Lanka, Thailand and Sumatra.

Typically eel-like in shape, this fish is easily identified by its characteristic markings. The dorsal part of the body is a rich brown, the belly yellowish. These base colours are overlaid along the flanks by a darker, irregular brown band that runs from the eye to the base of the caudal fin. This band branches alternately dorsally and ventrally to give the distinctive tyre-track patterning reflected in the common name.

M. armatus makes a welcome addition to the aquarium and, although it is somewhat secretive in its habits, it can be encouraged to venture out into the open to feed by reducing the tank lighting. It is aggressive

towards smaller fishes and even young specimens will quarrel among themselves and cause damage to fins if enough hiding places are not provided in the tank. Aquarium management is the same as that required for *M. erythrotaenia*.

Keep an eye on any wounds for signs of infection and take immediate action; these fish seem particularly susceptible to bacterial and fungal infections.

The tyre-track eel has not been bred in captivity. Fish caught in the wild during the spawning season show that mature females are more robust than males. In their native lands they are prized as a food fish.

MASTACEMBLUS ERYTHROTAENIA
Fire eel

Size: Up to 1m(39in).
Distribution: Burma, Thailand, Sumatra, Indochina and the Sunda Islands.

The dark grey body coloration of this very elongate fish extends into the finnage, and scarlet stripes run along the body, fading as they near the tail. The continuous dorsal, caudal and anal fins are edged in red.

Young specimens of the fire eel are quite gregarious but, as they mature, they become much more aggressive towards each other and require a great deal of space and several hiding places if they are to be kept in the same tank. Provide a substrate of fine sand with rounded grains; these fish love to bury themselves in the sand so that only the head is sticking out. They will also take up residence beneath pieces of slate on the substrate. Only well-established plants are safe in an aquarium inhabited by the fire eel, and even these may succumb to the excavations carried out when the eel requires a new lair. This habit of digging makes the fish susceptible to injury and, therefore, secondary fungal infections.

Mastacemblus erythrotaenia requires mature, well-oxygenated water, with a neutral pH and a general hardness of about 15°dH. A trickle filter system is ideal.

Young specimens feed on a variety of live foods, such as *Daphnia*, *Tubifex*, earthworms and mosquito larvae. As they mature, however, they require larger foods such as prawns and pieces of fish. In fact, these predatory fishes will eat anything small enough to fit into their mouths, although the aquarist may not witness this because of their nocturnal activity. Kept on their own, they become tame enough to hand feed.

In sexually mature fish, the females appear fatter than males, but there are no spawning reports for *M. erythrotaenia*.

Left: *It is unusual to see the whole of the eel-like shape of* Mastacemblus armatus, *as it spends so much of its time buried in the substrate or hidden beneath rocks and wood. Provide plenty of retreats and subdued lighting to make it feel at home.*

Right: Mastacemblus erythrotaenia *grows well in the aquarium on a diet of meaty foods. When young, offer the fish small live foods, but as they grow, they will need larger food items, such as shellfish and pieces of fish meat.*

INDEX

Index prepared by Stuart Craik

PICTURE CREDITS

Artists
Copyright of the artwork illustrations is the property of Salamander Books Ltd.

Rod Ferring: 10-11, 22, 23, 25, 26, 27, 28, 32-3, 45, 47, 48, 49, 55, 56, 75, 78

Photographers
The publishers wish to thank the following photographers and agencies who have supplied photographs for this book. The photographs have been credited by page number and position on the page: (B) Bottom, (T) Top, (C) Centre, (BL) bottom left etc.

David Allison: 17, 19(T), 30(B), 57(T), 60(C), 65(T), 73(T), 74(C), 82(T), 83, 95(T), 102-3, 103(B), 104, 109(BR), 111(T), 118(T), 124(B), 129(B), 137(T), 149(B), 151(T), 152

Berg/Bleher: 108-9(T)

Heiko Bleher: 117, 118-9(B), 119(T), 142, 142-3

Chaow/Bleher: 74(B)

Richard Crow: 132-3(B), 140

Dr. J. C. Chubb: 43(B), 44, 46(B), 48, 49(BL)

Max Gibbs: 38

J. Inge: 70(B)

Burkhard Kahl: 147

Koning/Bleher: 124(T)

Jan-Eric Larsson: 29, 30(T), 36, 37, 54(B), 66(B), 80, 88, 93(B), 94(T), 115(B), 116, 121, 146, 148, 150

Horst Linke/Bleher: 145

Hans J. Mayland: 66(T), 89, 105, 107, 112(T), 127, 130-1, 151

Mayland/Bleher: 61(BR), 72, 79(B), 112-3(B), 135, 138

Arend van den Nieuwenhuizen: 35, 54-5(T), 63, 68-9, 70(T), 71, 73(B), 76, 79(T), 81, 82(B), 115(T), 126, 153

Planet Earth Pictures: Title page(Kenneth Lucas), 58-9(Kenneth Lucas)

Hans Joachim Richter/Bleher: 19(B), 60(T), 110(B), 137(B), 144

Mike Sandford: Copyright page, 6-7, 16, 18, 21, 41, 43(T), 50-1, 52, 53, 56-7(B), 59(T), 61(BL), 62, 64-5(B), 67, 74(T), 77, 85, 87(T), 90, 91, 92, 95(B), 96, 97, 98, 99, 100(B), 106(BR), 108-9(B), 110(T), 123, 132(T), 134

Harold Schultz/Bleher: 100(T)

William A. Tomey: Half-title page, 8, 9, 13, 15(B), 34, 45, 46(T), 47(B), 49(BR), 84, 86, 87(B), 93(T), 94(B), 106(BL), 120, 129(T), 141, 149(T)

Brian Walsh: 15(T)

ACKNOWLEDGEMENTS

Publisher's acknowledgements
The publishers would like to acknowledge that the illustration on page 55 is based on one in *The Fresh and Salt Water Fishes of the World* by Edward C. Migdalski and George S. Fichter, published by Mandarin Publishers/Octopus Books Ltd., 1976/1977.

Authors' acknowledgements
Gina Sandford would like to thank Keith Banister, Heiko Bleher, Daphne Laylei and Brian Walsh for their help during the production of this book. Thanks are also due to her children, Jenny, Elaine and Rowan, for keeping a low profile throughout.

Richard Crow would like to thank the past and present members of the British Cichlid Association, whose queries and gems of information have greatly contributed to his knowledge of cichlids.